THE TESTIMONY OF JESUS

WITNESS LEE

Living Stream Ministry
Anaheim, CA • www.lsm.org

First Edition, September 2005.

ISBN 0-7363-2964-1

Published by

Living Stream Ministry
2431 W. La Palma Ave., Anaheim, CA 92801 U.S.A.
P. O. Box 2121, Anaheim, CA 92814 U.S.A.

Printed in the United States of America

05 06 07 08 09 10 11 / 9 8 7 6 5 4 3 2 1

CONTENTS

PREFACE

This book is composed of messages given by Brother Witness Lee in June and July 1975 in Seattle, Washington and Berkeley and Anaheim, California. These messages were not reviewed by the speaker.

CHAPTER ONE

THE LOCAL CHURCHES AS THE TESTIMONY OF JESUS

Scripture Reading: Matt. 16:18; Acts 4:11; Rev. 1:1-2, 9-13, 20; 19:7; 21:2, 10

The Bible contains three great matters: God's creation, God's redemption, and God's building. Concerning God's building, the New Testament contains the ministries of Peter, Paul, and John. The Lord first mentioned the building of the church in Matthew 16:18. When Peter recognized that the Lord was the Christ, the Son of the living God, Jesus immediately said, "I also say to you that you are Peter, and upon this rock I will build My church." The name Peter means "stone." From that day on, Peter was deeply impressed with the matter of building, and he became the first person after the Lord Jesus to speak about the building. Soon after the day of Pentecost, Peter preached that Christ was not only the Savior but also the cornerstone for God's building (Acts 4:11). Christ is the Stone-Savior, the Savior for salvation and the stone for God's building.

God's salvation is for God's building. In Christianity today people preach Christ mainly as the Savior, not as the stone, because most people have seen the matter of salvation but have missed God's building. In the past centuries, Christians have seen much concerning God's salvation. From the time of Martin Luther until the present, salvation has been made very clear to God's people. However, not many know about God's building. Salvation is not God's goal; God's building is His goal, and salvation is the process to accomplish the goal. The New Testament is a book of Christ, and it begins with Christ, but once people come to know Christ, He turns them to the building of the church. When Peter said, "You are the Christ," the Lord Jesus told him that he was a stone, and that He would build His church.

After the four Gospels is Acts, in which Christ is enlarged to be the builded church, and at the end of the New Testament there is a built-up city. In the first three chapters of Revelation there are the seven golden lampstands, which are the churches, and at the end of Revelation there is a city, New Jerusalem, as the consummation of the churches (Rev. 1:12, 20; 21:2, 10). This is according to the writings of John. In between Peter's speaking and John's writings is the ministry of Paul, which is mainly for the building up of the church as the Body of Christ (Eph. 1:22b-23a; 4:12, 16). By this summary we can see that the revelation of the New Testament is a matter of God's building.

The building of the church began with Peter's ministry, and it ended with Paul's. Why then do we need John's ministry? It is because after Paul's time the building was damaged. Therefore, we need the mending ministry of John. When John was called by the Lord, he was mending nets (Matt. 4:21). Many years later, his ministry became a mending ministry to mend the divine net. The way he mended the damaged net was with life. John brings us back to the beginning, to life, because according to history, the church was damaged by the religious doctrines, knowledge, and teaching of the Jews and the philosophy of the Greeks. Because both religion and philosophy are matters of knowledge, the mending ministry of John was to bring people back from mere knowledge, doctrines, teachings, and philosophy to life. John 1:1 and 4 say, "In the beginning was the Word...In Him was life." Knowledge damages and divides; only life mends and unites.

REVELATION BEING A PORTRAIT OF JESUS CHRIST

Revelation 1:1 begins, "The revelation of Jesus Christ which God gave to Him to show to His slaves the things that must quickly take place; and He made it known by signs, sending it by His angel to His slave John." The revelation of Jesus Christ is not merely an objective record revealed by Him; it is a subjective revelation. Objectively speaking, this book is the word of Christ, but subjectively, the entire book is a picture of Jesus Christ. The twenty-two chapters of this book are a single portrait. Verse 5 of chapter 5 says that Jesus is the Lion of the tribe of Judah. A painting of a lion may portray its life, history, and many other supporting characters. However, to speak of all the small characters is to miss the mark of the painting, since the painting as a whole is simply a portrait of the lion. Revelation with its twenty-two chapters is a "painting" of Jesus, portraying and depicting Him. However, if a painting portrays only the main subject without a background or environment, we would think that the artist is not very skillful. A good painter creates a picture full of meaning. Parts of the painting can cause us to weep, and other parts can cause us to rejoice. If a painting causes us to respond in this way, it is the work of the best artist. Revelation is this kind of "painting." The twenty-two chapters of this book are a good painting of the Lion of the tribe of Judah, but they also show an environment. Besides the Lion, there are beasts with horns and even a dragon (13:1-2, 11; 12:3). When John saw the situation in heaven, he wept, but when the Lion of the tribe of Judah came, there was great rejoicing (5:3-4, 8-14). Eventually, the Lion as the Lamb marries a bride, the bride becomes a square city, and the Lamb sits on the throne with God (19:7; 21:16; 22:1). Then out of this throne flows a river of water of life, bright as crystal, and in the river the tree of life is growing. What a picture this is! This is the revelation of Jesus Christ.

THE LOCAL CHURCHES BEING THE TESTIMONY OF JESUS

Revelation 1:1 says that God gave this revelation to show to His slaves the things which must quickly take place. If we know the revelation of Christ, we will realize that this is not merely a prophecy of events which will transpire in the future. Rather, these are all matters related to Christ, the divine Lion, and His many doings. Verse 2 says of John, "Who testified the word of God and the testimony of Jesus Christ, even all that he saw." Then verse 9 says, "I John, your brother and fellow partaker in the tribulation and kingdom and endurance in Jesus, was on the island called Patmos because of the word of God and the testimony of Jesus." Since I first came to the United States, I have considered speaking about the testimony of Jesus, but the time was not ripe to speak in this way. At this time, though, I am burdened to release this point of the truth. The testimony of Jesus is the enlarged Christ. A testimony of a person is something that gives us a clear picture of him. If someone looks at a picture of me, they will know the kind of person I am; this is my "testimony." In this universe there is a wonderful, mysterious person by the name of Jesus, but where is He today? He is in our city, but how can people see Him? No doubt, the local church, the church in each locality, is the testimony of Jesus today.

The testimony of Jesus is the practical church, not the church "in the air" or the church to come. A church yet to come cannot show Jesus to people, and a church "in the heavens" may show Jesus to the angels, but it cannot show Jesus to people on the earth. To show Jesus to the people in our locality, there is the need of a church in our locality that testifies who Jesus is. If someone in a locality wants to see Jesus, he must come to the church in that locality. Therefore, we need to consider whether we truly bear the image of Jesus. If we show someone an unclear picture of a person, it will not be a proper testimony of him with his image and appearance. We may see something in the picture, but it will not be the person we claim to show. The church in our locality must bear the image, expression, appearance, and virtues of Christ.

THE PRESENT AGE BEING NOT FOR OUR SPIRITUAL WELFARE BUT FOR BUILDING UP THE TESTIMONY OF JESUS

As an elderly man, I do not like to criticize or offend anyone. I prefer to love people and to be kind to them. However, when I contact God, I am burdened to speak concerning the situation in Christianity today. Christianity has mostly missed God's mark. Where is there a church today that truly bears the testimony of Jesus? Christianity mainly cares for people's salvation, joy, peace, and welfare—present and future. Because of this, if someone gives a message from the pulpit on the testimony of Jesus, he may be cast out. Many pastors, out of fear for their job, do not dare to speak concerning this. Due to this situation, fifty years ago the Lord was forced to go to the Far East, a heathen place, to find some young ones who did not care for their life but were charged with boldness to speak the truth to people.

This is not the age merely for people's salvation, peace, joy, and welfare. This is the age for the testimony of Jesus Christ. The more we are only for salvation and joy, the less we will enjoy them, and if we are only for peace, peace will not come. Even some pastors fight with their wives, and their children are rebellious. Where is the genuine peace? Because people are only for themselves, they lose everything. True salvation comes when we are for His testimony. There is no need to focus on our salvation. If we care for the testimony of Jesus, we will certainly enjoy salvation. People could martyr Peter and Paul, but they could never take away the apostles' enjoyment of salvation. Their enjoyment of salvation was secured by the testimony of Jesus.

We need to have a turn from our interest, salvation, peace, joy, and welfare. People in America may have better homes and cars than others have, but they do not have more peace, joy, salvation, or spiritual welfare. Today the Lord Jesus is seeking some people who will be for Him, some who will be bold and willing to say, "Lord Jesus, I do not care merely for my salvation from the lake of fire. I love You, and I want to be Your testimony." Anyone who says this will certainly be saved from eternal perdition. Likewise, whoever says, "Lord Jesus, I care not for my joy but for Your testimony" will be the most joyful person. The most joyful people are those who are for the testimony of Jesus. If we are not for Jesus' testimony, what kind of future can we have? Our future will only be one of getting old and weak and eventually being buried. There is no peace, joy, or welfare in this. We are not here for these things. We must be here for His testimony. We should say, "Lord Jesus, I do not care for my peace, my joy, my welfare, or my future. Lord, I care only for Your testimony here today." This testimony of Jesus is the local church, the church in our locality.

Whenever we touch the local church, we truly have joy, peace, and everything. After I came to the United States from China, I told my relatives and friends in China, "America is a good country, but it is good only for us to have the church life. If you are not for the church life, do not come here. It will be a terrible place to you." This country is the most sinful place, full of fornication, homosexuality, nightclubs, and many sinful things. There may be more evil here than in Sodom and Gomorrah. However, this is still the best place to have the church life. Here are all the modern conveniences, and people can make good wages simply by working in a trade. Many young Americans in the church life work only five days a week for eight hours a day, and then every evening they can come together to sing and praise the Lord. Some spend their entire Saturday and Lord's Day "churching" in the church life. To them, being in America is wonderful. One hundred years ago, to sail from the west coast of America to China took six months, but today we can fly to Taiwan in one day and come back the next day. We can also talk to brothers throughout the country and even throughout the world by a long-distance telephone call. Likewise, all the highways and freeways are for the church life. However, if the young people in such a top, rich nation are not for the church life, they will miss the blessing and fall into the "flood" of television, dancing, nightclubs, skiing, and surfing in this country. Like Noah and his family, we are here in the "ark" enjoying the presence of the Lord. This is the church life.

However, we should not care merely for our own enjoyment in the church life. If we do, we are fallen. We are here not for our own enjoyment but for the testimony of Jesus. As long as we are for His testimony, He will be our joy, but if we are for our own joy, we will have no joy. The Lord's testimony is our joy. Recently when I saw the young ones in a certain locality, I became very excited. They were so dear to me. I rejoiced so loudly that I had trouble with my voice afterward. Once when I was invited to speak to another small group, I spoke in a sad way, because everyone there was for himself; not one was for the Lord Jesus. That truly grieved my heart. On the contrary, I am very joyful to be with the churches in many localities. Sometimes my family cautions me to take care of my rest, but I cannot help myself. When I see the churches, I become excited. The church life is truly glorious because Jesus is testified here. The present revelation of God is not a mission or a work of preaching. It is to gain the testimony of Jesus in the church life.

THE SON OF MAN WALKING IN THE MIDST OF THE LOCAL CHURCHES AS HIS TESTIMONY

The first vision in Revelation is that of the seven lampstands, which are the seven local churches. The most impressive feature is that Christ is walking in the midst of the lampstands (1:13; 2:1). As a sign, this indicates that the place in which Christ can walk is the churches. If there were no churches on the earth, there would be no place for Christ to walk. To walk implies to appear to people. The place where John saw Jesus was in the midst of the churches. Many of us can testify that before we came into the churches, we knew of Jesus, but we did not see much of Him. In the church life, though, Jesus is here day by day. When we go to the church in each locality, there is Jesus. Jesus is everywhere in the local churches. In the churches we not only know of Jesus or hear of Him, but we see Him and meet with Him. What the Lord truly desires to gain is the local churches. Many Christians today are interested in knowing the prophecies. When we consider the situation in the Middle East, with Israel and the Arab countries, we can realize that these are the closing days of this age. We are very close to the end. However, the book of Revelation is not mainly a book of prophecies of the events to come. It is a book concerning the churches as the testimony of Jesus.

THE LOCAL CHURCHES BEING THE PLACE WHERE THE LORD WILL BUILD HIS CHURCH

As we saw, the Lord Jesus said in Matthew 16 that He will build His church, but where is He building His church today? He cannot build His church in a practical way in the Roman Catholic Church, amidst the masses, the burning of incense, and the confessions to the priests. Likewise, there is no way for the Lord Jesus to build His church in the large denominations. It is certainly possible for people to be saved there. Even in the Catholic Church many people have been saved. To some extent, those places are good for people to be saved, but we cannot honestly say that they are good for the Lord Jesus to build His church. What about the free groups or home Bible studies, that are composed of five to ten people who love the Lord and come together to pray and study? These are good for the sake of fellowship, but there is little opportunity for the Lord to build up His church in these groups. They do not intend to serve this purpose. If we go to them to try to speak something about the church, they may say, "Please, do not talk about this. You will only create trouble." There is also the so-called charismatic movement, even within the Catholic Church. In some Catholic churches we can find the "charismatic" things, the mass, and the worship of Mary all mixed together. Again, there is no way for the Lord to build His church in this situation. If we stand apart and objectively look at the situation, we will be clear that there is no way for the Lord to build up His church in the Catholic Church, the denominations, the free groups, or the charismatic movement. Where then can the Lord build up His church?

Over fifty years ago, in 1922, the Lord gained a young man, Watchman Nee, and burdened him concerning the church, and we all received the same vision through him. When I was under the good teachers of the Brethren assembly, I learned the Bible according to the letter, but I did not receive much revelation. At the same time, Brother Nee was used by God to raise up the churches. Eventually, I saw the vision of the church through his testimony, and I came out of the denominations. We were very clear about the church life. Once you see something, you can never say you have not seen it. From our youth we fought for the matter of the church, because we saw a vision of it. For the Lord's coming back, there is the need for the local churches so that the Lord may build His church. John 3:29 says, "He who has the bride is the bridegroom." We know that the bride is the church, but where in today's situation is the bride? Without the local churches, there is no possibility to have the bride.

As we have seen, the book of Revelation is not merely a book of prophecy concerning the beasts and the ten horns. It is a book of the church. In chapter 1 there are the local churches, and in chapters 2 and 3 there is more concerning the local churches. Of course, a good painting always has its background, so after the first three chapters there is something further concerning the world situation. Then in chapter 7 there is the great multitude of redeemed ones who constitute the church, in chapter 12 there is the man-child, the overcomers produced within the church, and in chapter 14 there are the one hundred forty-four thousand firstfruits and the crop, the harvest. In chapter 19 there is the bride who has made herself ready as the issue of the proper churches indicated in all the foregoing chapters; the bride in chapter 19 comes out of the churches in chapter 1. Finally, there is the New Jerusalem in chapter 21. Revelation begins with the seven churches and ends with the New Jerusalem, which is the consummation of the churches. All this is the testimony of Jesus.

If we truly mean business to follow the Lord, love Him, and be for His testimony, we all need to be clear that what the Lord needs today is the local churches. We do not criticize the other works that some do, but we realize that the central testimony that the Lord desires is the local churches. The local churches are all-inclusive. In the churches there are gospel preaching, outreach, increase, fruit-bearing, edification, the ministry of life, the growth of life, and the building up of the Body. The local churches are not a mission, work, denomination, or organization to maintain certain teachings and doctrines. The local churches are the expression of the all-inclusive Christ. Therefore, they are the testimony of Jesus. This will produce the bride, and this will issue and consummate in the New Jerusalem, which will be the full testimony of Jesus. In order to realize the testimony of Jesus, we must build up the local churches and then enter into them, just as Noah first built the ark and then entered into it. This is our salvation and testimony today, which is the testimony of Jesus. Here people can see Christ, and here Christ can walk, appear to people, visit people, and meet with people. This is the practical and living need for the Lord's testimony today. We must all see this, and we must all enter into it.

CHAPTER TWO

BEING ONE IN THE TRIUNE GOD FOR THE GLORIFICATION OF THE SON AND THE FATHER

Scripture Reading: John 17:1, 21-23; Rev. 1:11-12; Eph. 4:13

The proper church, as the testimony of Jesus, testifies that Jesus is unique. In our home, in our locality, in our country, and in the universe there is only one Jesus. John 3:29 says, "He who has the bride is the bridegroom." According to God's divine ordination, one husband has one wife. It is wrong for a husband to have more than one wife. Polygamy is not only sinful but ugly. A bridegroom and a bride are a figure, a picture, showing that in the entire universe, according to God's economy, there is only one Christ and one church. On the last night that the Lord Jesus was on this earth, He gave His final message, a long speaking of three chapters, John 14 through 16. These chapters are deep, living, rich, practical, and real. After this message, the Lord Jesus turned to the Father and prayed (17:1-26).

THE SON BEING GLORIFIED IN THE PROPER CHURCH LIFE THAT THE FATHER MAY BE GLORIFIED

The Lord's prayer was first for the Son to be glorified that the Father may be glorified (vv. 1-5). For many years, most of us have not understood this chapter. Almost all Christian readers of the New Testament realize that John 17 is a record of the Lord's departing prayer to the Father for the oneness of His believers. This is right, but only in a shallow sense. We need to consider where this oneness is and how it can be realized practically. Whenever we practice the genuine oneness, the Son is glorified that the Father may be glorified in the Son. The church life is the glorification of the Son; for the Son to be glorified there is the need of a proper church life (Eph. 3:21; 1 Tim. 3:15-16). In the Bible, *glory* means God's expression. We may illustrate this with electricity. Even though electricity has been installed in a building, no one is able to see it. When we switch on the lights, however, the electricity is seen. The shining of the lights is the "glorification" of the electricity. In the same way, Jesus Christ is a mystery, and it seems that no one can see Him. However, this Christ is expressed in the churches. Just as we know that there is electricity in a building by the shining of the lights, we know that Jesus is here by His "glowing" in the saints. Before His death the Lord Jesus prayed, "Glorify Your Son" (John 17:1). The intention, goal, and aim of this prayer were that the Father would build up the church for Christ. In this sense, *glorify Your Son* means "build up the church for Your Son." Practically speaking, the Lord's prayer in John 17 is a prayer for the church. The term *church* is not there in black and white letters, but it is there in actuality, reality, and practicality.

Just as electricity cannot be expressed without the shining of the lamps, the Son of God cannot be glorified without the church. When the Lord Jesus prayed, "Glorify Your Son," He was asking the Father to bring the church into being so that Christ may be expressed, that is, glorified, in His Body. In this way the Father is also glorified in the Son, because the Father is in the Son (14:10-11). If the Son is concealed, no one can know the Father, but when the Son is expressed, the Father is also expressed in the Son's expression. It is as if the Lord was praying, "Glorify Your Son in the church so that the Son may glorify You in His glorification." We also need to pray for the Son's glorification, His expression, in the proper church life today. When Christ the Son is expressed, the Father is expressed in the expression of the Son. We all need to see that the Lord's prayer to the Father in John 17 is a prayer, practically speaking, for the church life. Without the church life, how else can the Son be glorified? The Lord's prayer was fulfilled in Acts 2 on the day of Pentecost, when the Father through the Spirit raised up three thousand people and brought the church into being. It was at this time that the Son began to be glorified in the church, and in the glorification of the Son the Father was also glorified.

THE NEED FOR THE ONENESS OF THE BELIEVERS FOR THE SON'S GLORIFICATION IN THE CHURCH

For the Son's glorification in the church life, there is the need for the genuine oneness of all the Son's believers. This is why at a certain point the Lord Jesus turned His prayer to the oneness (John 17:6-24). If there is no oneness among the believers, there is no church life, and if there is no church life, there is no practical way for the Son to be glorified. The practical key for the Son to be glorified is the oneness of all the believers. This realization allows us to enter into the depths of the Lord's prayer in John 17. Practically speaking, it is a prayer for the church, and the church depends upon the oneness. The oneness is the crucial and basic item needed for the practice of the church life. The Lord Jesus foresaw this need, so He prayed ahead of time concerning this. On the one hand, the Lord's prayer for the churches was fulfilled on the day of Pentecost, but on the other hand, from that time to the present generation, division has been a problem in the church. The subtle enemy, Satan, knows that as long as the oneness is damaged, there cannot be a proper church life and the Son cannot be glorified in the church. Today we must realize that for the recovery of the proper church life, the first thing that must be recovered is the oneness among the believers.

My mother's grandfather on her mother's side was a Southern Baptist in the latter part of the nineteenth century, and my mother also was baptized as a Southern Baptist, although she was not saved. Then I was born as a fourth generation Southern Baptist. When I grew up, though, I made the decision to turn from my family's Baptist tradition to be a Chinese Presbyterian. However, I was still not saved. One day when I was nineteen, we heard an announcement that an evangelist, a twenty-five-year-old woman, was coming to our town to preach the gospel. According to the news, a thousand people were coming to listen to this young woman. I was stirred by this, and I wanted to see this preacher. I thank God for His sovereignty that one afternoon I went to hear her. Her message was on how Satan robs and usurps God's people, just as Pharaoh did. The preaching was powerful, and after only a short time, I was fully captured. I was an ambitious young man, endeavoring to finish my studies, but I was caught on that afternoon. I told God, "Even if You give me the whole world and make me a king, I would say, 'Thank You, but I do not want this.' I do not want to be usurped by Satan anymore. I want to go along with Jesus."

After this, I realized that the Chinese Presbyterian Church had nothing for me. I was hungry, and I wanted spiritual food. I loved the Bible very much. It was so sweet to me, like honey on the honeycomb. However, no one was able to present the Bible to me in a proper way. They did not know it in the way of life. They knew the Bible only according to its stories, but when I was young, my mother had taught us all the stories already. When she told us how Joseph was sold to Pharaoh, we shed tears, but now having been saved, I had received a new life, and the new life needed some new food. It was by this kind of seeking that I came into contact with the Brethren Assembly. They were famous for knowing the Bible, and this captured me. Therefore, I turned from the Chinese Presbyterians to the Brethren. I was fully satisfied there for a period of time. I sat there taking notes on the typology, dispensations, and prophecies, such as the ten horns, ten toes, four beasts, and seventy weeks (Rev. 13:1; Dan. 2:41-42; 7:3; 9:24). I heard over one hundred messages on the seventy weeks in Daniel 9. I was so happy because I came to know the Bible according to its prophecies, types, figures, and all the crucial portions of Daniel, Revelation, and Matthew. I continued in this way for seven years.

However, one day in August of 1931, as I was walking on the street, the Spirit within me checked with me, saying, "You have so much knowledge of the Bible, but look at how dead you are." That alarmed me very much. I stopped walking, looked to the heavens, and said, "Yes, I am so dead!" I wanted to shout, but I was afraid of offending people on the street. At that time I did not yet know how to call on the name of the Lord, so I waited until the next morning to go to a mountain not very far from my home. When I got to the top, I burst out and called, "O Lord!" and I wept and prayed. On that day I turned from the Brethren Assembly to life. Day after day for a long period of time I prayed to the Lord. In the following year, 1932, the Lord sent Brother Watchman Nee to my hometown, having been invited by the Chinese Presbyterian Church through me. That was the first time we met each other. After he came, he stayed in my home, and we had fellowship together. This was the first time I had met a man with the presence of Jesus and the flavor of the church life.

On the same day he left, a brother came to me late in the evening for fellowship, and we began to practice the church life in my hometown. I did not know anything about the proper church life. I had never been in a proper meeting of the church, and we did not even have a hymnal. Only we two, this one brother and I, came together on a Tuesday to begin to practice the church life, but on the second Lord's Day afterward, there were eleven young men coming together to partake of the Lord's table. Some sisters also insisted on coming, but we did not have the space for them because we had begun the Lord's table in my mother's living room. After being with the traditional American Southern Baptists, the formal Chinese Presbyterians, and the British Brethren Assembly, I turned to life, and in life the Lord turned me to the church. From that day in July of 1932 up to the present, which is now forty-three years, I have never had a regret or the thought to have another turn. There is nowhere left to turn. The next move will not be a turn; it will simply be a step into the New Jerusalem.

From that day we began to realize that the genuine church life depends inwardly on our honest and pure heart with a seeking spirit and outwardly on the oneness. The eleven of us who began to have the church life had come out of eight different denominations. Now we were in the heavens, praying, praising, and testifying mainly of our oneness. At that time, the Baptists were for baptism by immersion, the Presbyterians were for sprinkling, and the two were fighting with each other. However, at our Lord's table we praised the Lord for our oneness. We rejoiced over John 17 and said, "Lord Jesus, we are here as the fulfillment of Your prayer." Still, there were only eleven of us. The leaders in the denominations said, "Forget about these young men. They are merely boys at play." Nevertheless, from that day the church life became prevailing and stirred up the situation. This illustrates that in order to have the proper church life, the first requirement is the oneness.

OUR ONENESS BEING NOT IN DOCTRINE OR IN PRACTICE BUT IN THE DIVINE LIFE AND NATURE

The genuine oneness cannot be merely in doctrinal teachings. The more we are for doctrinal teachings, the more we will be divided. Neither is the oneness in our practices. Even today we do not know the best way to come together to meet and worship. We are not decided on the right way to sit, call on the name of the Lord, or pray-read, or whether to shout or be silent. We do not want to have a set way, because even the best things can cause a division if they are a set way. In the past, the Body of Christ has been fully divided both by doctrines and by rituals and practices. Therefore, from the beginning of the church life, we realized that we must beware of these two things. How then can we be one? We can see the way in the Lord's prayer in John 17. Verse 21 says, "That they all may be one; even as You, Father, are in Me and I in You, that they also may be in Us; that the world may believe that You have sent Me." The genuine oneness is the oneness in the Triune God—the Father in the Son and the Son in the Father—according to Their divine life and nature. We, the believers, are one not in doctrine or in practices but in the divine life and nature.

In Revelation 1:11 and 12, there are seven golden lampstands, one in each of seven localities. In typology, gold signifies God's divine nature. This means that all the believers in a locality are one in the golden nature of God. Each of us has a certain amount of the one divine nature, and we are one in this golden nature. However, if we come together to discuss the rapture, the tribulation, foot-washing, or head covering, we may quickly be divided. Even after a little doctrinal discussion we may lose the oneness. We can debate whether the bread on the Lord's table should be leavened or unleavened or presented whole or in portions, or whether the cup should have grape juice or wine, or whether there should be one cup or many. Some may ask how we have our meetings, who calls the first hymn, or whether or not we have a presiding pastor. The questions are endless. If we care for these things, we will soon be divided into many separate meetings. There is no way for the Lord Jesus to be glorified in such a circumstance. We need to declare that the Lord Jesus is the Head, the pure Word of God is the "shoulders," the divine nature is within us, and all the doctrines and practices are under our feet. In this way we will have the proper church life, the Son will be glorified, and the Father will be glorified in the Son's glorification. We cannot have the genuine oneness unless we are in the divine nature.

The Lord said, "That they also may be in Us" (John 17:21). Genuine oneness is in the Triune God who is dispensed into the believers. We should not care for mere doctrinal teachings. All the fundamental doctrines are good, but if we stand for doctrines, we will be divided. It is impossible to have the proper, genuine oneness through mere doctrines. Some may say, "If we do not care for doctrine, how can we keep the Christian faith?" However, the Christian faith is not a matter of foot-washing, head covering, or baptism. Some say that a head covering must be black, and others say it must be white. Some say that it must be long, but others say that since it is only a symbol, it can be small. There is argument after argument. Even those who practice baptism by immersion debate concerning how may times we should immerse someone. Some say we need to immerse a person three times, once in the name of the Father, a second time in the name of the Son, and a third time in the name of the Holy Spirit; otherwise, the immersion is not effective. Some also argue whether we should immerse in salt water or fresh water, in the sea, a river, a well, or in purified water, in a bathtub or in a swimming pool. Similarly, believers hold different opinions about the rapture. Some say it will be before the tribulation, some say after the tribulation, and some say during the tribulation.

All these considerations are not items of our Christian faith, and we should drop these kinds of arguments.

The proper Christian faith is first that the Bible is God's divine Word, divinely inspired by God, word by word. This is the first item of the faith, and if anyone does not believe this, he is short of the faith. Second, our faith is that our God is triune—one God as the Father, the Son, and the Holy Spirit. We do not have the mentality or expression to explain this, but the Bible tells us that it is so. We must believe that our God is such a God. He is not three Gods but one unique God, who is the Father, the Son, and the Spirit. Third, God the Son one day became flesh to be a man by the name of Jesus and lived on this earth for thirty-three and a half years. Then He went to the cross and died for our sins. He was buried for three days, and He resurrected physically and spiritually. Today the resurrected Lord as our Savior is in the heavens, and He is also within us (Rom. 8:34, 10). This is the most important item of our Christian faith. Fourth, we are sinners. Without believing in the Lord Jesus, we will perish, but by our believing in the Lord Jesus, our sins are forgiven and we have a new birth with the divine life; that is, we are regenerated. Then one day we will all be with our Lord for eternity. Moreover, all these believing persons, while they are on this earth, should come together to worship God in a corporate way as the church. These are all items of the Christian faith. No one can drop any one of these items; we must keep them all.

All other matters are simply different kinds of doctrines. Some are good, and some are not good. Some are fundamental, and some are not, but Romans 14 says that in order to have the proper church life, we need to receive every kind of genuine Christian, regardless of the doctrine or concept he holds. Some have different opinions and doctrines about food; some eat only vegetables, but others feel that everything is good for eating. Some say that every day is the same, but others believe that we should keep certain days as holy. These are examples of different doctrines and practices. In order to keep the oneness, we need to transcend all these things. However, if anyone does not believe that the Lord Jesus is the Son of God, he is not a Christian brother; he is in the principle of an antichrist (1 John 2:18, 22). Someone else may believe that the Lord Jesus is the Son of God, but that we are not saved by believing in Him; it is likely that such a person is also not saved. If someone simply believes that the Holy Bible is the divine Word; that God is unique and triune; that the Lord Jesus as the Son of God became man, died on the cross for our sins, resurrected from the dead to be our Savior, and is in the heavens and within us; that if we believe in Him, our sins are forgiven and we have eternal life; and that we all need to come together as the church, then we should not make an issue of his beliefs about the rapture, foot-washing, or head covering. Jesus prayed, "That they all may be one; even as You, Father, are in Me and I in You, that they also may be in Us." Our oneness is in the divine life and nature, not in anything else, and our oneness even is the divine life and nature. Therefore, when we fellowship, we should not ask one another about every manner of doctrine. We should forget about those things and simply praise the Lord that we are all brothers. We have one Father, one Lord, and one life, and we are one Body and one church in our locality. This is good enough.

BEING ONE IN THE GLORY, THE EXPRESSION OF THE FATHER

John 17:22 says, "The glory which You have given Me I have given to them, that they may be one, even as We are one." As we have pointed out, glory is the expression of God. Jesus seemed to be saying, "Father, You have given Me the life, the right, and the position to be Your Son in order to express You. Now I have given this glory to all My believers. They also have Your divine life, nature, right, and position to express You." This means that we are one in the divine expression. We are here not expressing a certain doctrine. We are here glorifying, expressing, God the Father. We do not stand for baptism, the presbytery, or even justification by faith. We receive justification by faith, and we practice baptism and the presbytery, but we are not standing for any of these. We are standing only for God. Our glory is not justification by faith, baptism by immersion, or the presbytery; our glory is God

Himself. We have the Son's glory, and in this glory, this glorious expression of God the Father, we are one. God is unique, His expression is unique, and His glory is unique. Therefore, we are unique in His expression. On the contrary, if we are for the presbytery, the charismatic gifts, baptism, or justification by faith, we are divided. We must all be for one unique expression, which is the glory of God the Father. In this way we are one.

BEING PERFECTED INTO ONE BY OUR GROWTH IN LIFE UNTO MATURITY

Verse 23 continues, "I in them, and You in Me, that they may be perfected into one." To be perfected into one is a matter of the growth in life. We may stand as one, but many of us are short of growth. This means that we are one but not yet perfected into one. Someone may say, "I care for the church life, but I am not happy with that certain brother." To feel this way indicates that we are not perfected. We are short of growth, and we need to grow. Ephesians 4:13 says, "Until we all arrive at the oneness of the faith and of the full knowledge of the Son of God, at a full-grown man, at the measure of the stature of the fullness of Christ." The way to arrive at the practical oneness is by the growth unto maturity. Even though we are in the church life, we may still murmur (Phil. 2:14). However, in the New Jerusalem there will no longer be any murmuring, because at that time John 17:23 will be fully answered and fulfilled. We need to be one, we must have the one goal to express God the Father, and we must have the growth so that we may be perfected into one. We have the divine nature for our oneness, the glorious goal of our oneness, and growth unto maturity for the perfection of our oneness. This is what we need, not a certain doctrine or practice.

Today we all have the divine nature within us, we have the one goal to glorify God, and we are all growing in life. Therefore, if we hear a young one, new one, or weak one complaining or murmuring, we should not be bothered. In a family, some little ones are still in diapers. We are not bothered by them. We simply clean them up, change their diaper, and let them grow. Every mother has the full assurance that after a few years the little ones will be out of diapers. God's family is a nursery with many little ones. This is wonderful, and we like to see this. We should not despise the little ones. The church is a family, not an army or a school. In a school all the students should be a certain age, but the church is an all-inclusive family. Likewise, we should not despise the older generation. We need the "grandfathers," and we must love them. They have more experience, and they can give good advice. We need to honor, respect, and praise the Lord for the older generation. It would be good to see many generations in the church.

A family is not a fighting army. However, the church must still be vigilant. To this end, we need the young people to fight the battle, just as a nation needs young soldiers for its defense. We need to respect the old ones, but we also need to raise up the young ones. Otherwise, we can have no peace. This is why 1 John 2:12-14 speaks of fathers, young men, and little children. This is the proper, all-inclusive church life. If we practice the church life in this way, there will be no divisions among us.

All of the above is according to John's mending ministry for the practice of the church life. Paul's writings contain many teachings, although, strictly speaking, he was not for those things. John, however, does not speak in the same way. He brings us back to God Himself, as in John 17:21: "That they all may be one; even as You, Father, are in Me and I in You, that they also may be in Us." He brings us back to the Triune God as our life and nature, our goal, and our growth in life. Today we have the proper church life. Now we must all be one to practice the church.

Chapter Three

COMING OUT OF RELIGION TO BUILD UP THE TESTIMONY OF JESUS

Scripture Reading: Rev. 1:1a; 12:1; 14:1, 4, 14-16; 19:7; 21:18-21; 2:9; 3:9; 2:20; 17:1-6; 2:13-14; 3:20; 18:4; Acts 2:40; Rom. 11:3-4

We thank God for the book of Revelation, the last book of the New Testament and the concluding book of the entire Bible. However, this book has not been opened to many Christians in a very clear way, and very few have truly seen its significance. Generally speaking, almost everyone considers this to be a book of prophecy. Whether this is right or wrong depends on our definition of *prophecy*. As we saw in a previous chapter, Revelation is not merely a book of predictions of events that will transpire in the future. Rather, in the nature of prophecy, it is a full revelation of Christ that opens the covering veil to give us a clear picture of this wonderful person (1:1a). In portraying Christ, this revelation also gives us a full record of the church from the first century until the time of the coming kingdom. Christ is in the church. In order to see who Christ is and what He is, we need to see the church throughout all the centuries. Then we can see Christ in the church, with the church, and in oneness with the church. This is a further view of Christ. Many Christians have seen the view of Christ presented by the four Gospels, the Acts, and the Epistles, but very few have seen Christ from the view presented in the book of Revelation.

Until around 1828, when the great teachers of the Brethren Assembly were raised up, including John Nelson Darby and others, the book of Revelation was mostly a closed book. On the one hand, these teachers opened this book in a general way, but on the other hand, they also misinterpreted certain matters. For example, Darby said that the scene around the throne in the heavens in chapter 4 takes place only after the church is raptured. He based this on the fact that John, as a representative of the church, was in the heavens in spirit (vv. 1-2). Then after the church is taken up, the tribulations follow as a judgment on the world. By moving directly from the historical churches in chapters 1 through 3 to the Lord's coming and the taking up of the church in chapter 4, this interpretation creates a gap of many centuries, leaving the book of Revelation incomplete. In our early days, we learned some things from Revelation through the writings of the Brethren teachers, but eventually we could not hold to any misleading concepts. Gradually as the years went by, the Lord showed us something further. The book of Revelation spans a long period of time, covering, in principle, all the things from the age of the apostles in the first century to the New Jerusalem in eternity.

The book of Revelation is a revelation not merely by Christ but concerning Christ in His church and in oneness with His church. Based upon this principle, it opens with the first three chapters depicting the situation of the church in a practical and full way. Later, in chapter 12 there is a wonderful, universal, pure, holy, and bright woman (v. 1). With her there is no darkness because she is clothed with the sun, the moon is underneath her feet, and on her head is a crown of twelve stars, which are the luminaries that shine in the whole universe. This woman is in contrast to Jezebel, the evil, ugly, dirty woman in Thyatira who seduces God's people to commit fornication and eat idol sacrifices (2:20-23). According to church history, Thyatira signifies the Roman Catholic Church. In the eyes of God, this church is Jezebel, who cheats the people who follow her. Some may ask, "Does not the Catholic Church teach people to worship God?" Yes, it does, but at the same time, it teaches people to worship idols. Over twenty-five years ago, while I was in Manila in the Philippines, I sought to know the facts about the Catholic Church, so I went to the largest cathedral there to watch and observe. Many people were worshipping idols. First, they went to a counter and bought a candle. Then they came into the cathedral, looked at all the idols, and considered to which one they should go. Most of them chose to go to the idol of the so-called "holy mother" to burn their candle, worship the idol, and pray to it. Under one idol was a notice that to come to it and pray every day would reduce a loved one's time in purgatory. This is to teach people to worship in God's name but in actuality to worship idols. This is evil and demonic, and it was prophesied in Revelation as Jezebel, the evil woman who teaches the Lord's servants to commit fornication and to eat idol sacrifices.

We should not be disappointed with chapters 2 and 3. Rather, we should go on to chapters 4 through 11 to arrive at chapter 12, where there is a woman not with idols but full of light—the sun, the moon, and the stars. Then from chapter 12 we go on to chapter 14, where there are the firstfruits and the harvest (vv. 1-5, 14-16). A little further on, however, the evil woman comes again as the great harlot, Babylon (17:1-6). Babylon is the consummation of the evil woman, Jezebel. With this great harlot there is a mixture. The New Jerusalem is a city of gold; the entire city proper is gold in nature (21:18), but the great Babylon is only gilded with gold, having a golden cup full of abominations. In appearance the cup is gold, but it is not gold within. This is a cheating, a deceit. The great harlot is gilded with the divine things, but we should not look only at the appearance. In the eyes of God, the cup is filled with abominations. This is a picture of the Catholic Church. From the outward appearance, it is gold, but inside are abominations. The harlot is gilded not only with gold but also with precious stone and pearls (17:4). In appearance, this seems to be the same as the New Jerusalem. However, the New Jerusalem is not gilded but built with precious stones and pearls on the base of gold (21:19-21). The Catholic Church is only gilded to deceive people with a good, divine appearance, but its contents are evil and abominable.

In chapter 2 there is Jezebel, in chapter 12 there is a bright woman, in chapter 17 Jezebel becomes a great harlot, and then in chapter 19 there is the wife of Christ (v. 7). Following this is chapter 21, which shows the New Jerusalem built with precious stones and pearls inlaid in the golden mountain. This is the wonderful picture presented by the book of Revelation, and in this picture we see Christ with the church and in the church. Therefore, as the revelation concerning Christ, the book of Revelation presents the testimony of Jesus, which is the church.

KNOWING THE AGE WE ARE IN AND THE PRESENT REVELATION OF GOD

We all need to know what age we are in, what the present revelation is from God, where we should be, what we should do, and what flow we should enter into. Time is short, and the day of the Lord's second coming is approaching. We must no longer be drugged by the religious things. We need to wake up to see where we should be and what we should do. This is a serious matter. The Lord Jesus likened this age to the age of Noah, saying, "Just as the days of Noah were, so will the coming of the Son of Man be. For as they were in those days before the flood, eating and drinking, marrying and giving in marriage...until the flood came and took all away" (Matt. 24:37-39). We must not be here unclear, drugged, and befuddled by the present situation. We must see what the age is, where we should be, and the way we should follow.

The Unbelieving World Being under God's Condemnation

Revelation gives us a clear vision of today's age and its prevailing flow and tide. If we spend time in this book with much prayer, the Lord will show us that the age today, from the unbelievers' side, is full of evil and corruption. We will see that on the whole earth the age is full of evil matters, such as fornication, adultery, sodomy, dancing clubs, robbery, and violence. There is no hope for this age. God does not have any thought to cure it but has already given up on it. The unbelieving world is now under God's condemnation and judgment.

Judaism Being the "Synagogue of Satan"

In addition, on the earth today there are three typical religions. I do not count Confucianism, which contains only ethical teachings and is not a religion. I do not even count

Islam, because it is an imitation, a counterfeit. The Islamic holy book, the Koran, is merely a counterfeit of the Old Testament with a little of the New Testament. The Koran even says something about Jesus, whom it calls "Isa." According to the Koran, Isa was merely a great servant of God who was neither crucified nor resurrected. When Isa was about to be crucified, God took him to Himself in heaven. Then one day this Isa will return to continue his human life. What a counterfeit this is! The typical, genuine religions are Judaism (the Jewish religion), Catholicism (Romanism), and Protestantism. Do you love these three "isms"? No, we simply love Jesus.

It was under Judaism that Jesus was brought into the world. However, in speaking to the churches, the Lord mentioned the "synagogue of Satan" (2:9; 3:9). Synagogues are places of worship for the Jews, but those synagogues became the synagogue of Satan. In the eyes of God, all the synagogues of the Jews are synagogues of Satan. Although the Jews teach people to worship God, God is not in the Jewish synagogues today. Rather, Satan is there. This is the view not of man but of God. We must all realize that God is frank; He never pretends. On the contrary, Satan is always subtle and never frank. The first time Satan came to man, he came as a small serpent. Adam and Eve were not aware that this serpent was Satan. He always comes to us pretending to be something better than he is. He is evil and ugly, but he comes as something that appears nice. This is Satan's way. One day Satan came to the Lord Jesus in this kind of subtle way. In Matthew 16:16, Peter recognized the Lord Jesus as the Son of God, and the Lord Jesus praised him for that. Right away, however, this same Peter who had received a revelation from the Father became one with Satan (vv. 21-23). Satan came through Peter to frustrate the Lord Jesus. If the Lord Jesus had not had the insight, He might have been cheated. Of course, He did have the insight, so He rebuked Peter, saying, "Get behind Me, Satan!" The Lord Jesus saw through him. Apparently that was Peter, but actually it was Satan. In the same way, apparently the synagogues of the Jewish religion are for the worship of God, but in actuality Satan is there. They are the "synagogue of Satan."

Catholicism Seducing God's People with Idolatry and Heathen Practices

As we have seen, the Catholic Church is Jezebel. People in Catholicism worship Jesus, but they worship Mary even more. At the entrance to a cathedral in Manila is a statue of Mary, one of whose hands is almost completely worn out. When I asked the people there what had happened, they told me that every day hundreds of people would come to touch that hand and that over many years this had worn it out. What a superstition this is! Catholicism teaches people something about Jesus, and they teach people to worship God, but their teachings are, for the most part, misleading.

In the Catholic churches today there is the so-called charismatic movement, in which speaking in tongues, the worship of Mary, and the Catholic mass all come together. What a confusion! Catholicism is subtle. As long as people belong to the Catholic Church, it accepts almost all the things they bring in. When the Catholic missionaries went to China, the Chinese people were practicing ancestor worship, and it was very hard for them to give this up. Because of this, some of the priests asked the pope to allow Chinese Catholics to continue this kind of worship. They were afraid that if the Vatican did not allow it, almost no Chinese would come into the Catholic Church.

Catholicism contains many heathen items. When Catholicism went to the Philippines, all the natives had their form of idol worship. Many of these forms were collected by Catholicism and added into their worship. For example, at a certain time each year there is a feast day, a special day of repentance. Before that day, people may rob from one another, but on the day of repentance they would repent of what they did. After the feast day, however, they would begin again to steal.

Protestantism Retaining Subtle Things Related to Idols and Being Dead

What then of the Protestant churches? To the church in Pergamos the Lord said, "I know where you dwell, where Satan's throne is" (Rev. 2:13). Satan's throne indicates his kingdom. Then verse 14 mentions the teaching of Balaam, which is to teach God's people to eat idol sacrifices and to commit fornication. This does not pertain to the Jewish centers of worship, the synagogues, and it is not found only in the cathedrals of Catholicism. This teaching is also found in the Protestant churches. Some may argue and say that they never saw idols in the Protestant churches. However, we should be careful. There are some idols there. The title Reverend, for example, is an abomination to God. Only God Himself is to be revered. This is a small indication that should open our eyes to see that in Protestantism there are subtle things related to idols. As a sign, the church in Sardis prefigures the Protestant church, from the time of the Reformation to the second coming of Christ. In the eyes of God, the reformed church is dead (3:1). Moreover, even though certain matters were restored by this church, these things were about to die; hence, they needed to be revived (v. 2). This is the actual situation of the Protestant churches.

Our Need to Come out of Religion and Be Saved from This Crooked Generation

Today there is the unbelieving world. In addition, there are the things that belong to the enemy of God, including idols, Satan's synagogue, Satan's throne, and deadness, that are related not to the unbelieving world but to the religious world—Judaism, Catholicism, and Protestantism. Where then should we be today? Should we be in the unbelieving world, going to movies, skiing, dancing, surfing, and gambling in the casinos in Reno and Las Vegas? Should we go to Judaism or Catholicism? Should we be "Reverends" in Protestantism? On the day of Pentecost, Peter told the Jewish people, "Be saved from this crooked generation" (Acts 2:40). At that time, the crooked generation did not refer mainly to the unbelieving world but to the Jewish religion (Gal. 1:4). Do not ask, "Is there no God in Judaism? Is there no Christ in Catholicism and no Jesus in Protestantism?" Yes, the name of God is in Judaism, the name of Christ is in Catholicism, and the name of Jesus is in Protestantism. However, Satan is also there. God, Christ, and Jesus are there in name, but Satan is there in actuality.

Therefore, under the covering of the Lord's prevailing blood we say, "Come out of her, My people" (Rev. 18:4).

According to Revelation, there is a fifth category. Besides the unbelieving world, Judaism with its synagogues, Catholicism as Jezebel, and Protestantism, there is the pure church life and a call to the overcomers (2:7, 11, 17, 26; 3:5, 12, 21). The wrong concept about overcoming is that we need to overcome the small things, such as bad habits, our temper, smoking, or drinking. According to the context of chapters 2 and 3, however, to overcome is to overcome the evil, crooked, and perverse generation of Judaism, Catholicism, and Protestantism. Some among us, who were Jews, have overcome Judaism. However, in front of the trap of Judaism there are two snares. One is called Catholicism and the other, Protestantism. Some may come out of Judaism, but if they are careless, they will fall into one of these two snares.

Every religion today is a "drug," a deceit, but the book of Revelation shows a clear, pure, bright, and shining way. We must take the way of the "sun," the "moon," and the shining "stars" (12:1). We must not be drugged and deceived by things that have the appearance of godliness. Those are not the genuine articles. We must all come out of those things. We must be clear, honest, and faithful; otherwise, we will be fully befuddled and judged by the Lord with this generation.

THE WAY OF THE LORD'S RECOVERY TODAY

The Lord Reserving a Remnant for Himself

The United States is a Christian country. Today there are millions of genuine Christians here, saved, washed with the blood, and regenerated in their spirit. There is no need to ask concerning the unbelievers or nominal Christians. Among even the genuine Christians, how many are truly here for God's eternal purpose? Many of them are only for their own welfare. With many, it is difficult to discern whether they are Christians. Their homes, cars, clothing, and appearance are all the same as those of the unbelievers. It is difficult to discern who are the children of God and who are the children of the devil. Nevertheless, we do not believe that our God is doing nothing in this age today. Instead, we fully believe that our God is working strongly on this earth to attract a remnant of His lovers and seekers. Elijah once went to the Lord to accuse the Israelites, saying, "Lord, they have killed Your prophets, they have torn down Your altars; and I am left alone, and they are seeking my life." The Lord answered him, "I have reserved for Myself seven thousand men who have not bowed the knee to Baal" (Rom. 11:3-4). We in the church life are a reserved people.

Some may think that if the Lord's recovery is of God, we will have a great movement and gain a large number of people. If we do this, though, we are not the Lord's recovery. The Lord's recovery is always on the narrow way. In the ancient time, Noah preached righteousness for one hundred twenty years, but he gained only eight persons, including himself. No doubt Noah had many relatives, but only his wife, three sons, and three daughters-in-law entered with him into the ark. That was God's way in Noah's age. The Lord Jesus worked for three and a half years with many kinds of miracles, but eventually He gained only one hundred twenty persons (Acts 1:15). People today like to trust in miracles, but the Lord Jesus even raised people from the dead, and still only a few believed. There will be no great movement in the Lord's recovery today. Rather, there will be a small number. The seekers and lovers of the Lord must be pure in their motive, heart, and goal toward the Lord. These are the ones reserved by God for the fulfillment of His purpose.

The Lord's Recovery Being Fully Separated from the Crooked, Perverse, and Condemned Generation

The entire world, with its unbelieving and religious aspects, is condemned by God. God is using His faithful seekers in His recovery to protest against today's trend. Therefore, it is a shame for someone to be in the Lord's recovery yet still go to movies and bear the signs of modern fashions. The people in the Lord's recovery should be the reserved ones, fully separated from this crooked, perverse, and condemned generation.

The church life is the recovery of the testimony of Jesus, which is the testimony that the Lord Jesus lived as a human being on this earth, not by Himself but by His Father. He could proclaim to the entire universe that the subtle one, Satan, God's enemy, had nothing in Him (John 14:30). The whole world is under Satan, yet this man had nothing to do with Satan, and Satan could do nothing with Him. He lived this kind of victorious life on the earth by His Father (6:57a; 4:34; 5:19, 30; 7:18; 14:10). The church is the testimony of such a Jesus. When the church people walk on the street, not only the angels but even the worldly people can discern that we are a separated people. We have nothing to do with the unbelieving world or the Jewish, Catholic, or Protestant religions. We care only for the living Jesus. He is our life, and we live by Him and for Him. This is the testimony of Jesus, which is the proper church life.

To be sure, nothing is a legality in the church life. There are no regulations posted on the wall concerning the way the brothers should cut their hair or the way the sisters should dress. The church life is simply the testimony of Jesus. This Jesus, the One who lived by the Father's life and in whom Satan had nothing, is in us today. All religions care for regulations, but the church cares only for Jesus. We have no regulations or rituals but a living Jesus who lives in us. We do not ask anyone to care for regulations. Rather, we help them to care for the indwelling Jesus by telling them that Jesus is their life, He lived on the earth by the Father's life, and Satan had nothing in Him.

We too must have such a life, a life having nothing to do with the world or with any kind of religion. We do not care for ways of baptism, head covering, rituals, speaking in tongues, or manifestations of gifts. All these belong to the religious world. We care only for the living Jesus. Some say that if we do not speak in tongues or have healings, we do not have the spiritual gifts. However, the first gift in 1 Corinthians 12 is the word of wisdom, not speaking in tongues, and the second gift is the word of knowledge. The last two of the nine gifts mentioned are speaking in tongues and interpretation of tongues (vv. 7-10). To emphasize tongues and interpretation is to turn the gifts upside down, making the tail into the head. In every meeting we have words of wisdom and of knowledge. Who can say that we have no manifestation of the gifts? Nevertheless, we do not care for the gifts. We care for the living Jesus. If we care for gifts, we are in religion. We are not here for any religion; we are here for Jesus.

As the children of Israel wandered in the wilderness for forty years, they saw the greatest miracle every morning. The heavenly manna came to at least one million people every morning. If such a thing happened today, people would come from all around the world to see it. However, this great miracle accomplished nothing inwardly for those people. Out of one million people, only two, Joshua and Caleb, received the genuine help. According to John 2:23-25, the Lord Jesus would not commit Himself to those who were interested in miracles. God can never trust this kind of person. He trusts only in those who have a pure and single heart toward Him.

THE CHURCH LIFE BEING TODAY'S ARK TO TERMINATE THE PRESENT AGE AND BRING IN GOD'S KINGDOM

Today is not the age of miracles or of gifts. Today is the day of the living Jesus, and God wants a people who live by this Jesus. These people will be today's Noah, who terminate the present generation and usher in the coming age, the age of the kingdom. This is what the Lord is doing today. The Lord's work is not a matter of right or wrong doctrine. His work is to attract His lovers and seekers who have a pure motive with an open spirit to follow Him in an absolute way so that He may have the church life to protest to the whole world against the present trend, terminate this present age, and bring in God's kingdom. This is God's purpose that He is fulfilling today. We look to the Lord that in the local churches in many places this revelation will become clearer and clearer, day after day and week after week, so that we will all see what the Lord wants today. The Lord desires "the family of Noah" to build the ark and testify against the trend of the age so that He can use them to terminate this age and bring in the kingdom age. What we are building in the church life is today's ark for our salvation (Phil. 2:12) and for the salvation of the ones under our care.

CHAPTER FOUR

WORKING OUT OUR OWN SALVATION FROM THE RELIGIOUS AGE

Scripture Reading: John 15:19; Acts 2:40; Gal. 1:4; 6:13-15; Phil. 2:12-16

According to the revelation of the Gospels, the Lord Jesus was born not into a Gentile world but into a religious world. His mother Mary was in the Jewish religion, He was raised near the center of that religion, and when He came out to minister, almost everyone He met was a member of that religion. Because of this, while the Lord Jesus was on this earth, He had two categories of disciples. One was those who were in the Jewish religion but followed Him out of the fold, the "camp" (John 10:1; Heb. 13:13), such as Peter, John, James, and many other young ones. The other category was those who believed in Him but remained in that religion, such as Nicodemus, an honest, faithful disciple of Jesus who did not follow Him out of the camp (John 3:1; 7:50-52). The old prophetess Anna was also for the Lord Jesus, but she probably did not follow the Lord to leave the temple (Luke 2:36-37).

Most of those who followed the Lord were young ones. Moreover, the elders in the first local church on the earth, the church in Jerusalem, were all young people. When the Lord Jesus first came out to minister, He was only thirty years old. Although Peter may have been the oldest of the first disciples, he still may have been a few years younger than the Lord. In this case, he would have been in his late twenties. For this reason, we are glad to see many young ones in the local churches. It is easy for young people to believe in the Lord Jesus and follow Him out of the old fold, the old "camp," but it may be more difficult for the older generation to follow Him out.

Nicodemus and Joseph of Arimathea, two older disciples, took care of the Lord's body and buried Him in a new tomb (John 19:38-41). However, despite what they did for the Lord, they did not openly display their belief in the Lord and were probably not among the one hundred twenty in Acts 1. They were honest believers of the Lord, but they were not in the church in Jerusalem in practicality. Some may argue, "Were they not members of Christ?" Yes, Nicodemus and Joseph may have been members of Christ, but we must not consider the church in a merely doctrinal way. We need to deal with the actual situation. Whether or not they were members of the Body in reality, they were not in the church in practicality. Rather, they were still in the old fold, which was not only forsaken by the Lord but also condemned by Him.

RELIGION BEING A SUBTLE FRUSTRATION WITHIN US

In one sense Peter was clear about the old Jewish religion, because he faithfully followed the Lord Jesus and was the leading apostle and elder to set up the first local church in Jerusalem. However, even he was not as crystal clear as Paul was concerning the Jewish religion. Even after the day of Pentecost, at the time of Acts 10, Peter was still holding on to the old concepts of Judaism, which forced the Lord to repeat His vision to him three times (vv. 9-16). Peter said, "By no means, Lord," but the Lord was patient with him until he finally saw the vision concerning Cornelius's household. Later on Peter was still weak. What is recorded in Galatians 2:11-14 transpired after Acts 10. In Acts 10 he saw a clear vision from heaven that God was through with Judaism, but he was still able to act as he did in Galatians 2, appearing to keep the ordinances of Judaism. Because the apostle Paul could not bear this, he rebuked Peter to his face. However, when Paul went to Jerusalem for the last time in Acts 21, even he was defeated by the influence of Judaism. It is difficult to believe that an apostle like Paul, who condemned Judaism to the uttermost in his Epistles, went into the temple and paid the expenses for four men to keep the Jewish rituals (vv. 23-26).

He was convinced and subdued by the Jewish religion. The Lord could not go along with this, so after Paul paid the expenses for their vows, the Lord stirred up the situation with the people, and it was through this that Paul was put into prison. Not long after this, in A.D. 70, the Lord sent the Roman army under Titus to destroy the holy city and the holy temple, leaving no stone upon another (Matt. 24:1-2). The Lord could not tolerate to see His believers still for the things of Judaism, which had been condemned. This demonstrates that religion is a great, subtle entanglement that has been planted deeply into all of us. The element of Christianity has gotten into our blood, and it is difficult to get rid of it.

BEING SAVED FROM THE CROOKED GENERATION, THE RELIGIOUS WORLD

The Lord Jesus used the word *world* a number of times in the Gospels. Many Christians hold the understanding that this refers only to the secular world. In fact, *world* many times refers to the religious world, that of Judaism. The Lord said, "If you were of the world, the world would love its own; but because you are not of the world, but I chose you out of the world, therefore the world hates you" (John 15:19). The Lord chose His disciples out of Judaism, the Jewish religion. When the Lord said that the world hated the disciples and that they were not of the world, this did not mean that the disciples were not of the Gentile world. Rather, it meant that they were not of the Jewish religious world. In Acts 2:40 Peter said, "Be saved from this crooked generation." That generation was of the Jewish religion. The Jewish religion was the crooked generation from which those Jews needed to be saved on the day of Pentecost. In Galatians 1:4 Paul says that the Lord Jesus Christ "gave Himself for our sins that He might rescue us out of the present evil age," which is the religious world. In 6:13-15 Paul speaks of the world being crucified to him, and he to the world. Many Christians misapply these verses, supposing that *world* refers to the secular world. According to the context, though, *world* is a matter of circumcision, which is a religious ritual. The proper meaning of these verses is that on the cross the Jewish religion was crucified to

Paul, and Paul was crucified to it. It is so good that today also many are being saved from the religious world, the present evil generation.

RELIGION BEING SUBTLY UTILIZED BY SATAN TO HOLD BACK GOD'S PEOPLE

God has a purpose, but Satan is subtle, creeping in to utilize and usurp what God has done. God chose two peoples, Israel and the church. God used the Old Testament for the fulfillment of His purpose, but Satan subtly utilized it to form Judaism in order to hold back Israel from God's purpose. Then in the New Testament time, God used the church to fulfill His purpose, but the subtle one crept in again to utilize and usurp the New Testament, forming a Christian religion to hold back Christians from fulfilling God's purpose. Now Israel is held back by the Jewish religion, and Christians are held back by the Christian religion. Eventually no one is left to fulfill God's purpose.

UNHEALTHY MESSAGES DAMAGING THE BELIEVERS' PROPER APPETITE

Much of what is being ministered in Christianity today may be considered either as a drug or as candy. According to a proper diet, neither drugs nor sweets are good. Sweets damage the appetite. A proper wife will care for her husband by restricting his eating of desserts. The husband may not be happy with this, but he should realize that this is good for his health. Eating desserts without proper food damages the appetite and creates bad behavior. The more sweets a child eats, the worse his temper is. Children acquire bad behavior from eating too much candy, but when their mothers stop feeding them candy, the children become well-behaved again. In addition to bad temper, high blood pressure and heart problems are also made worse by eating too many sweets. A country that is too rich in desserts will have a high rate of heart attack and blood problems. This is an illustration of the situation in Christianity today. Even the fundamental churches minister too many "sweets" to people. They have changed the appetites of the believers until even the real believers care to eat only "candy" and have no appetite for solid food. Anyone who comes to minister solid food offends them, because they have no capacity to digest and assimilate it. They know how to drink only sweet, soothing milk. In our early days, we very much appreciated a devotional book entitled *Streams in the Desert,* which compiles quotations from Charles Spurgeon and others for the purpose of comforting the reader. However, this book may be considered as a "dish of candies," one for each day of the year. We eventually realized that the sweet and soothing nature of this book damages the appetite, causing the reader to care only for hearing comforting words and not to know how to receive unveiling words.

We may illustrate the shortage related to this kind of book in the following way. A Christian husband and wife with different natural dispositions may discover that they are not very suitable for each other, but because they are Christians, they cannot divorce; instead, they will both suffer. If they read a devotional book, however, they will be comforted. The husband may read a portion that says that although his wife is not submissive, she is still good for him; his situation will be a help to him and will accomplish something for him. Apparently this is a good word to comfort the husband. However, such a word will also strengthen his disposition. It will not expose his natural make-up or unveil his natural disposition. Mrs. Jessie Penn-Lewis, however, was a writer of another category. She taught that God's intention is not merely to give comfort to people but to put them on the cross. However, if the husband in our illustration were to hear these words, he would not be able to receive them, because his appetite has been fully accustomed to hearing only sweet, comforting, soothing words as "candy" to be eaten day by day, year after year. Who can fulfill God's purpose today? Many of the messages in Christianity contain either the drugs of heresy or sweet candy.

RELIGION BEING THE TOP FRUSTRATION TO THE FULFILLMENT OF GOD'S PURPOSE

The Lord now needs some to rise up to speak unveiling words. This is what the Lord Jesus spoke. He was born into the Jewish religion, but when He came out to minister, He offended many people. He did not drug anyone nor did He sweeten them. Rather, He came to people with God's purpose, telling them not only of God's salvation but also of God's way to fulfill His purpose. This offended all the Pharisees. Eventually, the ones who persecuted Him were not the Gentiles but the Jewish religionists. The persecutors of Jesus were pious religionists, who sentenced Him to death according to their religious law. Therefore, the world that hated the Lord Jesus was not the Gentile world, the secular world, but the Jewish, religious world. It was the same with the apostles. It was the high priest of the Jewish religion and those with him who put Peter into prison (Acts 5:17-18), and it was the religious Jews scattered in the Gentile world who persecuted Paul. Wherever Paul went to preach, the Judaizers followed him to stir up opposition (13:44-45; 17:5). The principle today is the same. As I have been in this line of ministry for over forty years, I have not been persecuted mainly by unbelievers. Almost all my persecutors from the first day up until today have been Christians. Likewise, the persecution against the local churches in the United States does not have its source in the Gentile world. In every locality, the persecution comes from the source of Christianity.

EATING AND DRINKING JESUS TO BE HIS COMPANIONS IN THE FULFILLING OF GOD'S PURPOSE

This shows that not only is it impossible to fulfill God's eternal purpose in religion, but religion is the top frustration to God's purpose, whether it is the Jewish religion or Christianity. Religion may help people a little, but this religious help always turns into a frustration. Religion is a system that teaches people to worship God and behave in a good way in order to please God, apart from Christ. While teaching people to worship God and to behave in order to please God, religion keeps people away from the real experience of Christ. God's intention is to work Christ into all of us that we may be the partners of Christ to fulfill God's eternal purpose. Only those who partake of Christ can be His partners, His companions, to fulfill God's eternal purpose (Heb. 1:9; 3:14). However, Satan is subtle, using the typical, scriptural religion to keep people away from experiencing Christ. This is why the Lord Jesus tells us in Revelation 2 and 3 that we do not need the teachings, doctrines, regulations, rituals, and rites of degraded religion. We need only to taste, eat, partake of, and enjoy the Lord Jesus as the tree of life and the hidden manna (2:7, 17). To eat is to take something outside of us into our being. Day by day we need to take the Lord Jesus into our being. The significance of the Lord's table is that in our remembrance of the Lord we declare that we live and have our daily life by eating and drinking Jesus, who is our life and life supply. Day by day we live by Him, so on the first day of the week we come together to testify to the whole universe that eating and drinking Jesus is our way of living.

BEING DELIVERED FROM THE RELIGIOUS ELEMENT WITHIN US

First we must come out of religion, and then we must get religion out of us. We need to jump out of the snare of every religion: the Jewish religion, the Catholic religion, and the Protestant religion. Then we must expel all the religious elements out of us. To some degree, we all hold on to some religious element. If a brother comes out of the Jewish religion, the element of the Jewish religion may remain unconsciously, subconsciously, and deeply within him. This will cause trouble for his fellowship in the Body. Likewise, some dear brothers who have come from certain Christian backgrounds still retain that element within them. This also bothers them and frustrates the proper fellowship. Someone may love the Lord and come out of religion to be a good brother in the church life, but a certain amount of the religious element may still be planted deeply into his organic tissues. In such a case, the religious element will always rise up at a certain point. No doubt, we have come out of religion, but has the religious element been radically, fully, and thoroughly eradicated from our being? If it has, then we will never be troubled in our fellowship in the Body.

WORKING OUT OUR SALVATION TO BE SAVED FROM THE PRESENT GENERATION AND TO FULFILL GOD'S PURPOSE

We must learn not to hold on to anything religious. We must drop every bit of religion and enjoy Christ. In all things we need to enjoy Him and eat Him as our food. He said, "I am the bread of life," and "he who eats Me, he also shall live because of Me" (John 6:35, 57). Every day we need to eat Him as the bread of life, the tree of life, and the hidden manna. This should not be a mere doctrine to us; it must be practical. We need to forget about the teaching of Balaam, the teaching of Jezebel (Rev. 2:14, 20), idol worship, and all the worthless things of religion and eat the tree of life, eat the hidden manna, and even feast with the Lord Jesus day by day (vv. 7, 17; 3:20). This will help us to build up our salvation. Philippians 2:12 says, "Work out your own salvation." This is not the salvation that saves us from eternal perdition. It is the salvation that saves us from the crooked and perverse generation. We need to work out this salvation.

We need not be bothered by this word, because verse 13 tells us that God is now operating in us both the willing within and the working without for His good pleasure. Because God's operation motivates us within, we simply cooperate with Him to work out the salvation that saves us from the present generation. To have the proper church life is not only to stand on the ground of oneness but also to build the ark, like Noah's family did, to save ourselves from the present evil generation and bring us into a new age. We need this kind of salvation, one built not by God directly but by our daily cooperation with His inward operation. This is the revelation of God today.

We should not argue and say, "Can I not stay in the Catholic Church? Are not the Presbyterian and Baptist Churches also the church?" These are not proper questions. The proper consideration is what the Lord's way is to fulfill His purpose, terminate the present age, and usher in His kingdom. We have offended certain ones by saying that there is no possibility for the Lord to build His church in the Catholic Church, the denominations, the free groups, and the charismatic movement.

However, we have no intention either to offend anyone or to please anyone. Our intention is only to please God. We need to tell people the truth. The revelation from God today is that we all need to work out the salvation that will save us from the crooked generation, terminate today's age, and bring in the kingdom age so that God's eternal purpose will be fulfilled. This is not a matter of our welfare—our peace, joy, or going to heaven. It is altogether a matter of satisfying God by fulfilling His eternal purpose. Dear ones, this is the age for us to walk with God (Gen. 5:22; 6:9). By walking with God, we build the ark that will save us and others to fulfill God's purpose by terminating the old age and ushering in the new age. This is God's revelation today, which we need to see. For this purpose, we do not need rituals or regulations. What we need every day is the Lord Jesus as our food, the tree of life, and the heavenly manna to sustain us, support us, encourage us, and strengthen us so that we can take this higher way. Day by day we must walk on this way for the fulfillment of God's purpose.

CHAPTER FIVE

THE TESTIMONY OF JESUS BEING THE CHURCHES AS THE GOLDEN LAMPSTANDS

Scripture Reading: Rev. 1:1-5, 9-13; 12:17; 19:10; 3:14; Exo. 25:31-32, 37

THE BOOK OF REVELATION BEING THE ULTIMATE CONSUMMATION OF THE DIVINE REVELATION

As the last book of the Bible, Revelation is the ultimate consummation of the divine revelation. Even in human writing and speaking, the last word is important. The Bible is a long story with sixty-six books, but without the final book we would miss very much. If we read only Genesis through Jude, we would be lost, knowing neither the goal, destination, nor completion of the Bible, nor the ultimate revelation of God Himself. We must all see that this book is crucial to our Christian life, especially in the end times.

Unveiling God's Eternal Purpose to Have a Building

God's eternal purpose is to have a building. The Bible opens with creation, but it closes with a city. This tells us that God's work began with creation and will consummate with a building. Genesis 1:1 says, "In the beginning God created the heavens and the earth," but at the end of the Bible what we see is not merely a new heaven and new earth. If the entire universe were only the heavens and the earth, it would be empty. We may prefer the heavens, but if God's goal is not accomplished there, they are empty. It is on earth that there will be something that attains to God's goal. Therefore, at the end of the Bible there are three new items: the new heaven, the new earth, and the New Jerusalem (Rev. 21:1-2). If we were to enter into the new heaven and new earth without the New Jerusalem, we would need to weep. Without the New Jerusalem we would have no home in the new heaven and new earth, no city or building where we can meet with the Lord. Strictly speaking, God will eventually be neither in the heavens nor on the earth but in the New Jerusalem. The New Jerusalem is His final goal. This demonstrates that in order to know God, we need to know the book of Revelation.

Presenting the Revelation of Jesus Christ

To some extent, Revelation contains teachings and prophecies, but it is not merely a book of teachings and prophecies. The first two verses of this book tell us that it is the revelation of Jesus Christ. Among Christian teachers and Bible students there is much dispute about the small phrase *the revelation of Jesus Christ* in 1:1. Some say that it refers to the revelation given by Christ. However, this phrase means that this book is the revelation concerning Christ; it is the unveiling of Christ Himself. The word *revelation* refers to the opening of a curtain or veil. If a person has a veil over him, we will not be able to see him, and the more we try to study him, the more we will not accurately know him. This illustrates the situation in today's Christianity. The book of Revelation is meant to be an unveiling, but the more people read it, the more they are veiled. Up until this day, many among us may still not see what is in this book. Some may say that this book tells us about the beasts and how one has ten horns and seven heads (13:1-2, 11). Others may see that the seven lampstands are the seven churches, but they do not know why the churches are signified by lampstands (1:12, 20).

In the book of Revelation we should see only one figure, Jesus Christ, because this book is the revelation and unveiling of Jesus Christ. As we have said before, we may compare this book to a painting. We may have a painting of a lion, but in order to bring out the figure of the lion, we need a background and an environment. The best paintings always have a good background and environment. The main figure in the book of Revelation is Christ as the Lion of the tribe of Judah (5:5), but in order to present this wonderful Lion, Revelation has a certain background and environment. In the first vision of this book, the Lion is walking in the midst of the seven lampstands. At this point, though, He is not in the form of a lion. As He is walking in the midst of the lampstands, He is the High Priest (1:12-13). Later, many other characters come into the picture. In chapter 12 there is a wonderful woman (vv. 1-5). It is difficult to tell where she is, because she is clothed with the sun, the moon is underneath her feet, and a crown of stars is on her head. After this, a serpent creeps in (v. 9), and then there are two beasts (13:1-2, 11). All these "characters" are a wonderful environment for the "painting." Eventually, after traveling through a long journey, the Lion is enthroned in the center of the New Jerusalem as the King of kings and Lord of lords. This is the "painting" of the divine Lion in the book of Revelation. If we have seen this painting, then we will know what we are and where we are. We are not the creeping snake or one of the beasts. We are the golden lampstands.

Knowing Christ Not Only As the Redeeming Lamb but Also As the Overcoming Lion

Some Christians focus on the serpent, the beasts, and the woman and miss Christ. They study the background but miss the main figure of the painting. We need to see the unveiling of Christ in the book of Revelation. Every Christian knows the Christ in the four Gospels, but very few see Him in the book of Revelation. The Christ in the book of Revelation is different from the Christ in the four Gospels. The Gospel of John says that He is the Lamb (1:29). Revelation also says that He is the Lamb, but it tells us something further. He is no longer only the Lamb; He is now the Lion. The Lion is not the same as the Lamb. Is our Christ today the Lamb or the Lion? We may say that He is the Lion, but in our experience He is still the Lamb. In Revelation 5 the angel introduced Him as the Lion of the tribe of Judah, but when John turned to see Him, he saw a Lamb (vv. 5-6).

Today He is no longer only the Lamb. In the four Gospels He is the Lamb, but in Revelation He is the Lamb-Lion. If we love the Lord, He is the Lamb to us, but to those who do not love Him He is the Lion. He is the Lamb to us and the Lion to the enemy, the world, and the sinful things. Since we do love Him and He is the Lamb to us, why must He also be a Lion? It is because there are still many negative things in us. He died on the cross as the Lamb of God to redeem us, but even after being redeemed, we are still mixed with many negative things. Therefore, He must also be the Lion to deal with these things.

In the Gospels, John could recline on Jesus' bosom. John was close to Him, and He was nice, dear, gentle, kind, and loving to John. However, when John saw Him again in Revelation, he was frightened and fell at His feet as dead (John 13:23; Rev. 1:17). Out of His mouth proceeded not words of grace but a two-edged sword (Luke 4:22; Rev. 1:16). In John, Jesus looked at people and wept; He truly captured people by His loving look. In Revelation, though, His eyes are like a flame of fire, burning and shining (John 11:35; Luke 22:61; Rev. 1:14). Therefore, we have the full freedom to say that the Christ in Revelation is different from the Christ in the Gospels. We all need to see this different Christ.

CHRIST BEING THE TESTIMONY OF GOD

Revelation 1:2 mentions "the testimony of Jesus." The testimony of Jesus is the full revelation of Christ. I have been ministering in the United States for over twelve years, and I have spoken of many matters. However, throughout these years the time was not right to minister fully concerning the testimony of Jesus. I have spent much time to obtain the proper understanding of the testimony of Jesus, and for many years this was a mystery to me. Some would say that the testimony of Jesus is our living as He lived. He was meek, humble, kind, and gentle, and when we live in this way, we are a witness to Him. Forty years ago I accepted this kind of interpretation, but eventually I realized that it was not adequate. The same Greek word in the New Testament is translated both as *testimony* and as *witness*. A testimony is a witness. The main difference is that the latter can be used as a verb, meaning to bear witness, or testify. When used as nouns, *testimony* and *witness* can refer either to the thing testified or to the person who gives the testimony. Jesus is the testimony of God, expressing God to men. All men know that there is God, but no one has ever seen Him. However, there is a man in this universe, who was even on the earth, by the name of Jesus, who was and still is the testimony of God. Whatever God is, we can see in Him (John 1:18). Jesus testifies God not only by His word and deeds but by what He is. His very being is the testimony of God.

THE CHURCHES BEING THE TESTIMONY OF JESUS

However, God now needs an enlargement of His testimony, which is the church. Christ is the testimony of God, and the church is the testimony of Jesus. What God is, is fully expressed in Jesus, and what Christ is must be fully expressed in the church. Both the Old Testament and the New Testament speak of a golden lampstand. In Exodus there was a single, unique lampstand (25:31-40). This typifies Christ as God's testimony, shining as the divine light in the darkness. In the New Testament, however, there is no longer only one lampstand but seven (Rev. 1:11-12, 20). The lampstands are no longer singular but plural, no longer individual but collective. Now God's testimony is not an individual matter but a corporate one. Seven signifies completion and perfection. In Revelation we have the completion of the lampstand. In the Old Testament the lampstand signified Christ individually, and in the New Testament the seven lampstands signify the churches in a corporate way. God's testimony in the Old Testament was individual, but in the New Testament it is corporate. Even in the Old Testament there was an indication of something plural in the lampstand. The one lampstand had six branches, three branches on each of two sides, and seven lamps. This signifies that the unique Christ would branch out to become sevenfold. In the Old Testament Christ was uniquely one as the lampstand with seven lamps. Then in the New Testament there are seven lampstands, signifying that the one unique

Christ has branched out. Just as He is the testimony of God, the churches are His testimony.

Revelation 1:1 and 2 reveal that this book is not only the revelation of Christ but also a record of the testimony of Jesus. As such a record, this book speaks concerning the churches. Verse 9 says, "I John, your brother and fellow partaker in the tribulation and kingdom and endurance in Jesus, was on the island called Patmos because of the word of God and the testimony of Jesus." Immediately after this, John received the vision of the seven lampstands, the local churches, with the wonderful Christ walking in their midst (vv. 11-13). This is the vision of the testimony of Jesus. Therefore, the local churches are the testimony of Jesus.

The Lampstands Being of Pure Gold, Signifying the Divine Nature of God

This testimony is of pure gold. In typology, gold signifies something marvelous. Gold may be considered as the purest of the elements. Moreover, nothing can damage gold. Regardless of what we do to a piece of gold, it remains the same. Gold can withstand every kind of dealing, trial, and hardship. In addition, gold never rusts. Because of this, gold signifies what God is in His divine nature. God is pure; He is purity itself. Nothing in this universe is as pure as He is. Revelation 22:1 speaks of a river of water of life, bright as crystal. Sometimes in a message we can sense the water of life, but the water is not clear and pure. For this reason, while I am speaking, I often look to the Lord and say, "Lord, speak the pure word through me." Only God is purity.

God can also never be damaged. Consider how many trials Jesus passed through and the temptations He suffered. Eventually, nothing was able to damage or change Him. We, however, are not like this. In my ministry in the past I saw many good young men. Beginning in 1933 I came to know a group of young Christians in my home province of Shantung, who were all students in the medical college there. At that time they loved the Lord. I loved them, and they invited me to speak to them several times. However, after not more than ten years, all those dear ones changed. When they were students, they went on well with the Lord, but after their graduation they changed. Some changed because of their medical practice, and others changed because of their marriage. In the United States I also saw some promising ones, but eventually they also could not withstand the snares of their job or marriage. There is no need to mention other things; even a job or marriage can change us. Sometimes even owning a car changes a brother, and an item of modern fashion from the department store changes a sister. A sister may truly love the Lord, but she may not be able to stand against the temptations of modern fashions. We are too changeable. While Jesus was on this earth, all manner of things happened to Him, but He was always the same. With Him there was never a change. This is because He was the testimony of God.

Moreover, Jesus never "rusts"; that is, He can never be corrupted. Because we are all constantly "rusting," we need the meetings to "polish" us up again. If we do not come to the meetings for two weeks, we will collect much rust. I too need the meetings. I mostly speak one night a week; all the other meetings I attend in order to be polished, since I also suffer from the flesh. Rusting is mainly due to dampness. On the one hand, our spouse and children are like fire to burn us, but on the other hand, they are like dampening water to cause us to rust. We rust because we are not divine; we are merely human. Even copper, which is similar to gold, rusts. There is only one element that never rusts, that is, God as our gold.

Now we can see why the testimony of God is a golden lampstand, and the testimony of Jesus today is the golden lampstands. The genuine testimony is something that is absolutely divine, not altogether human. If our love is altogether human, it will rust after a short time. Our human love is polluted and even evil. It can be compared to copper or bronze that seem good but rust. The testimony of Jesus must be golden, that is, divine. This is possible because He has worked Himself into us. We must all see that what God wants is not mere human beings. We should not say that we are right or good in anything. Whether we are right or wrong, or good or bad, does not make a difference, just as whether a piece of copper shines or rusts makes no difference. The problem is that it is only a piece of copper. What God wants is not us, the copper, but Himself, the gold. A wife and husband may often fight. In this kind of fighting, every husband says that he is right, and every wife vindicates herself. Those who have not seen that whether we are right or wrong makes no difference will always vindicate and fight. We are merely "copper," and sometimes even "mud." Even if we are completely right, we are still not golden. What God wants is the gold. To see this is the secret to not fighting with our wife or husband. If we have seen that what God wants is not what we are, we will not fight or vindicate ourselves, because we will realize that what we are—right or wrong, good or bad—means nothing. What counts in the eyes of God is only Himself.

The Testimony of Jesus Being the Corporate Lampstands

However, the testimony of Jesus is not simply one piece of gold. Instead, it is the lampstands. One person is not a lampstand. Only the church is a lampstand. If we remove a piece of gold from the golden lampstand, the piece is still golden. In nature and element it is the same as the lampstand, but it is not the lampstand. Only the lampstands are the testimony of Jesus. Today many Christians consider that as long as they are spiritual, holy, and for the Lord, everything is all right. However, it is not all right. What God wants today is not separate pieces of gold. What He wants is the corporate lampstands. We must all become the lampstands.

Our burden is to see the Lord's present revelation and what He wants us to be. The Lord's present revelation is concerning the recovery of the proper church life. Wherever we are, we must be in the church. If we are not in the church, we are not the testimony of Jesus, regardless of how golden we are. The testimony of Jesus that the Lord desires today is not only golden but is the golden lampstands. We are not qualified by ourselves to be the testimony of Jesus. We do need to be golden, spiritual, and up to God's standard, but we also must be built into the church. The testimony of Jesus is not a single piece of gold. It is the built-up corporate lampstands.

The Testimony of Jesus Being the Proper, Recovered Church Life

I am very burdened about this because I have heard much criticism concerning the church for the past forty to fifty years, even up to the present time. Nevertheless, we must not miss this vision. I do not care about the criticisms, because I know by the pure revelation of the Word that nothing but the church is the testimony of Jesus today. Someone may be more golden than others, but if he is not in the proper church life as a built-in part of the church, he is not in the testimony of Jesus. In the book of Revelation, the testimony of Jesus is not individual Christians. The testimony of Jesus is the local churches. If there is no proper church where we are, we should spend every penny and even our own being to be in a place where there is a church. Likewise, if we are in a place where there is a genuine church, we must never stay away from it. If we stay away from the church, we will miss the mark of the Lord's testimony. If anyone does not believe this today, one day he will admit that this is true, but it may be too late. We would not like to see this. We would like to see that each person is in the testimony of Jesus.

We are golden, but we are not merely pieces of gold. Rather, we must all be able to say firmly, strongly, and positively that we are the golden lampstands. As long as we cannot say this, we are through. We may love the Lord, be for the Lord, be spiritual, and know the Bible more than others, but if we are not the golden lampstands, we are not the testimony of Jesus. What the Lord desires today is the testimony of Jesus. Those who love the Lord Jesus may have had many experiences according to the Gospels and the Epistles, but they should go on from there to the book of Revelation. According to the last book of the Bible, what the Lord wants is the testimony of Jesus.

Without entering into Revelation, we have no goal. In this case, we may be good Christians, but we are wandering Christians. The proper goal is the church. To say that the goal of our salvation is for us to go to heaven is according to a shallow concept of the New Testament. Rather, we are saved for the church, we love the Lord for the church, we preach the gospel and win souls for the church, and we seek spirituality for the church. There is nothing wrong with seeking spirituality, but spirituality that is not for the church means nothing. Everything must be for the church. What the Lord wants today is not all these other things but that we would be the church.

Many people have attacked me and said that I am too much for the church, even addicted to the church, but we can never be too much for the church. We need to see the vision of the church. Once we are caught by the vision, we would not change. For over forty years I have never changed my tone concerning the church. Those who have listened to me again and again for all these years can testify to this. I cannot say that I have not seen the vision. I have seen the testimony of Jesus, and I came to this country with a vision. What the Lord Jesus wants today is the testimony of Jesus, which is the local churches as the pure golden lampstands, the proper, recovered church life.

CHAPTER SIX

BEING SAVED FROM THE CROOKED GENERATION TO BE THE TESTIMONY OF JESUS

Scripture Reading: Rev. 2:1-7, 8-11, 12-17, 18-20, 24; 3:9, 12, 17-18, 20; Acts 2:40; Gal. 1:4; Phil. 2:12-13, 15

God's goal in His creation of man was to have a corporate expression of Himself. According to this goal, man was made in the image of God in order to be His testimony (Gen. 1:26). This means that man was destined to be the expression of God. Because Adam failed God in this respect, Jesus came as the second man (1 Cor. 15:47b) to take the position and function of Adam. Thus, the living person of Jesus is the expression, image, and testimony of God (Col. 1:15). In the same way, the church today is the testimony of Jesus, that is, His expression. In the first chapter of the Bible, man is in the image of God to express God, and in the last two chapters of the Bible there is a building, the New Jerusalem, to express God. According to the book of Revelation, God on His throne has the appearance of jasper, and the New Jerusalem also has the appearance of jasper (4:2-3; 21:11, 18). This means that the entire city is God's expression in His image. By this we can see the consistency of the Bible from the beginning to the end.

THE DESTINY OF MAN BEING TO EXPRESS GOD IN A CORPORATE WAY AS HIS UNIQUE TESTIMONY

No doubt, there is the matter of our personal salvation in the Bible. We were all lost, and we must believe in the Lord Jesus to be saved. To a certain extent, we also need to seek the Lord to improve our living and conduct. However, this is not God's consistent goal. God's consistent goal is to have a unique expression of Himself. Neither the sun by day nor the moon by night can express God. Even the myriads of angels are not qualified or destined to express God; they are simply His servants (Heb. 1:13-14). In the whole universe, only man has the destiny to express God. The meaning of man is that he is to be the expression of God. Man was created not merely to be saved, to go to heaven, or to be a good person with good behavior. Simply to be saved and have a certain behavior are far off from God's consistent goal. We were all created in the image of God with the destiny of expressing God.

Moreover, the expression of God according to His consistent goal is not individualistic but corporate and collective. We may claim to be expressing God, but it may be in an individual way, not in a corporate way. From the first page to the last, the Bible reveals that what God desires as His expression is corporate. God commanded the Israelites to build only one tabernacle. At that time over a million people were traveling in the wilderness, and that small tabernacle was only thirty cubits long and ten cubits wide, smaller than a common meeting hall (Exo. 26:15-16, 18, 20, 22-23). Nevertheless, that small tabernacle was the unique center for the worship of God. As such, it was the unique expression of God. Since God is one, He did not want to have more than one tabernacle among His people. God is omnipresent, but He does not desire to be omnipresent in that way. We can never divide God's expression. God is uniquely one, so His expression must also be uniquely one. Similarly, there was only one temple of God in the ancient times. Since there were twelve tribes, it seems logical that each tribe should have had one temple, just as in modern times the United States has fifty states, each with its own legislature. However, our modern wisdom is not superior to God's wisdom. All the twelve tribes had only one temple, because God's expression is unique.

Likewise in the New Testament, there is only one church, because there is only one Christ. In the Old Testament there were three unique things: one God, one tabernacle, and one temple. In the New Testament there are also three unique things: one Christ, one church, and one holy city, the New Jerusalem. When I was in Jerusalem in 1958, I went to see the spot where, according to tradition, Jesus was buried and resurrected. Upon this site is a building, and at various corners of it are sections belonging to different major denominations. This is a picture of the division among Christians. Nevertheless, there is one God, one tabernacle, one temple, one Christ, one church, and one New Jerusalem.

CARING MORE FOR THE TESTIMONY OF JESUS THAN FOR OUR OWN SALVATION AND SPIRITUALITY

God's intention is to have a corporate expression. Before I was saved, I was a fourth generation Christian in name and by tradition. As a child I was indoctrinated, drugged, and befuddled with every kind of concept from Christianity. Apparently these concepts were according to the Bible, but in actuality they were not. For many years I heard the preaching of pastors, ministers, and missionaries, but no one ever told me that we must be the corporate expression of Christ on the earth today. God desires an expression in this universe, and wherever this expression is, in each locality, it must be uniquely one.

John says, "I John, your brother and fellow partaker in the tribulation and kingdom and endurance in Jesus, was on the island called Patmos because of the word of God and the testimony of Jesus" (Rev. 1:9). Almost all Christians today would say that they are for the word of God, but very few will say that they are for the testimony of Jesus. We are here not only for the word of God but also for the testimony of Jesus. Immediately after John declared this, he saw a vision of the seven lampstands, signifying the seven local churches (vv. 10-12, 20). The central concept of the first three chapters of Revelation is the seven lampstands as the seven local churches to be God's expression. We must not think that God has changed His mind today. From the first page through the last, the Bible as the Word of God is always consistent concerning the one God, one tabernacle, one temple, one Christ, one church, one local church in each locality, and one New Jerusalem.

Many Christians desire to be heavenly and spiritual. However, the angels are the most heavenly and spiritual beings, having neither the flesh nor troublesome minds to bother them, but they are not the testimony of God as His expression. They are only His servants to minister to those who are to inherit salvation (Heb. 1:13-14). The testimony of Jesus is the church. According to most of the teachings in Christianity, the church is simply the gathering of the many saved ones who are ready to go to heaven. This definition is poor and is according to a fallen concept. A number of years ago in Taiwan, certain leading ones in Christianity rebuked me, saying, "You should not say that today's Christianity is fallen." I responded, "If today's Christianity is not fallen, then what is? As long as any of us are not up to God's standard, we are fallen." Christianity impresses people mainly with personal salvation, at best. It does not convey any revelation concerning the testimony of Jesus. If we are in the testimony of Jesus, we do not need to focus on our personal salvation. Our salvation is secured by being in the testimony of Jesus.

The testimony of Jesus today is the church. This is not merely our own concept. If we read through all the sixty-six books of the Bible, we will come to the last book, Revelation. This book does not speak concerning personal salvation and personal behavior. The crucial matter in this book is the testimony of Jesus. We need not worry about our salvation. As long as we are a part of the testimony of Jesus, we are saved. Likewise, we should not worry about our holiness, spirituality, or any other matter. If we are a part of the testimony of Jesus, we will have everything.

THE TESTIMONY OF JESUS REQUIRING US TO LOSE OUR SELF-IDENTITY, CONCEPTS, AND TASTES IN ORDER TO BE BUILT UP WITH OTHERS

To be the genuine testimony of Jesus will cost us everything. Can we say that we are the testimony of Jesus? If we were the testimony of Jesus, we would not be able to be worldly, and we would not be able to argue much with our husband or wife. To not quarrel, in itself, does not constitute us to be the testimony of Jesus, but anyone who is a part of the testimony of Jesus cannot remain in a quarrel with his wife. Likewise, a brother in the testimony of Jesus will not be able to have improperly long hair (1 Cor. 11:7, 14). As long as a brother still has improperly long hair, he is not practically a part of the testimony of Jesus. If he loves all of the saints and behaves himself in a humble, nice, and kind way, we may consider him to be a good brother. However, the fact that his hair is too long is a sign that he is still holding on to his taste, which means that he cannot be built together with the saints. To cut our hair is a small thing in itself. What is crucial is that whoever holds on to his own taste needs to be crucified with Christ. It must be "no longer I" with my tastes (Gal. 2:20). We must not hold on to anything. The "I" with our concepts and tastes must be over. If this is the case, it will be easy to be built with all the saints.

Someone may seem like a good brother in the church, but in what way is he good? Is he simply gracious, a good husband, and one who comes to all the meetings? Instead, a brother must be "good" in being built up with others. We have learned a lesson from observing "good" brothers. Sometimes the nicest ones are the strongest ones to dissent. The nicer someone is, the more difficult he may be to deal with. This is because many good ones are natural and hold on to their concepts and tastes. They love the Lord and the church, but they never lose their individual identity to be built up with others. Different pieces of gold may be round, square, or rectangular, but when they are beaten together into one golden lampstand, they lose their identity. In the building up of the church, we all need to lose our identity. Otherwise, we may still be pieces of gold, but we are not the golden lampstand.

We must all see that what the Lord desires today is not wonderful pieces of gold, even the best pieces. Someone may be a wonderful piece of gold, but in a sense, this is his problem. Simply because he is so wonderful, he would not be built up with others. We need to say, "Lord, have mercy upon me. I do not want to be 'wonderful.' I do not want to be the best one, and I do not want to be anything special. I want only to be built up in the church. Lord, I wish to lose my identity to be a part of the lampstand." To be the lampstands as the testimony of Jesus is the goal of God's eternal purpose, and this is our destiny. As long as we are in the golden lampstands, we surely are saved, and it is here also that we become holy, spiritual, heavenly, and divine.

To be a part of the testimony of Jesus costs us our everything, but in actuality all that we are and have are nothing. We are nothing, and we have nothing. To be the testimony of Jesus requires us to be lost and nullified. What God wants today is the testimony of Jesus, which is the local church. Every local church is a lampstand, bearing Christ as the lamp shining for God. Someone may come to the meetings, but he still may not be built in. I have seen certain good saints who were in the church, but later they stayed away from the church. Revelation 3:12 says that the pillars in the temple "shall by no means go out anymore." Once we are built into the temple as a pillar, we can never get out. If we could pull ourselves out of the church, it means we have never been built into it. The only way to take out a part of a building is to tear down the whole building. If we mean business with the Lord to have the local church, we can never get out of the building.

THE EPISTLES TO THE SEVEN CHURCHES IN REVELATION REVEALING THE CONDITION OF JUDAISM, CATHOLICISM, PROTESTANTISM, AND THE WORLD

Revelation 2:1-7 speaks concerning the church in Ephesus. This church had good behavior, strong faith, and many works for the Lord. However, it was rebuked for not enjoying the Lord adequately. The church in Ephesus had lost the enjoyment of the Lord. We know this from verse 7, in which the Lord says, "To him who overcomes, to him I will give to eat of the tree of life, which is in the Paradise of God." To eat of the tree of life is to enjoy the Lord. The peril and danger today is that we may have good behavior, strong faith, and many good works for the Lord, but we may not enjoy Him very much. The Lord does not care how much we do for Him. He cares for how much we eat Him and enjoy Him daily. He is the tree of life for us to eat.

In the past, I heard many messages charging me to have

good behavior, strong faith, and do many works for the Lord, but I never heard a message telling me that I need to eat the Lord Jesus. We may have done many works for the Lord, but how is our enjoyment of Him? Do we enjoy the Lord Jesus day by day? Every morning the first thing we should do is eat the Lord Jesus and enjoy Him. We all need to forget about what we do for Him. Instead, we need to enjoy Him. Nothing pleases Him as much as our eating Him. The more we eat Him, the happier He is.

Verses 8 through 11 speak of the church in Smyrna. Because the church there suffered persecution, the Lord spoke nothing against them. In this epistle is the first mention of the synagogue of Satan (v. 9). A synagogue is a place where the Jews worship God, but the synagogue has become something of Satan. This indicates that Judaism had become something satanic, the synagogue of Satan. In this same principle, the cathedrals, chapels, and sanctuaries of Christianity today are also not truly something of God. The third church is the church in Pergamos (vv. 12-17). Here is the place where Satan's throne is (v. 13). The place of Satan's throne is the place where Satan is the king, ruling and reigning over the world. In other words, in the church in Pergamos there is the world. Pergamos signifies the worldly church, the church that is married to the world. It is difficult to discern many of today's Christians, since they appear the same as the unbelievers. In their shopping, housing, and dress they are the same as the people in the world. Many Christians are worldly, dwelling in the place where Satan's throne is, the place where he dwells. Judaism is satanic, and worldliness also is satanic.

In the fourth church, the church in Thyatira, there is the woman Jezebel (vv. 18-29), signifying the Roman Catholic Church. Just as Judaism is satanic, the Catholic Church today is demonic. The Jews do not worship idols in their synagogues, but the Catholic cathedrals are full of idols. I spent much time to study the situation in Catholicism. When I was in Manila, I visited a Catholic cathedral there. I was surprised to see all the idols. Under one idol, an image of a certain saint, was a note, saying that if someone prays to her several times a day, the sufferings of a relative in purgatory would be relieved. What a superstition this is! It is demonic. Frequently in these places there is also the idol of the "holy mother." Can we say that those Catholic cathedrals are something of God? They are not only satanic but also demonic. Verse 20 says that Jezebel teaches and leads the Lord's slaves astray to commit fornication and to eat idol sacrifices. Fornication is an evil "sister" of idolatry. Where there is idolatry, there is always fornication.

The second through fourth epistles in Revelation 2 speak of Judaism, worldliness, and Catholicism. In chapter 3 we come to Protestantism. Verse 1 says that although the church in Sardis has a name that it is living, it is dead. The characteristic of Protestantism is deadness. Furthermore, verse 20 says, "Behold, I stand at the door and knock." This is not the door of individual persons; it is the door of the church in lukewarmness, which we also see in today's Protestantism. We need to realize that the Lord is not in Protestantism; He is outside the door. Therefore, Judaism is satanic, Catholicism is demonic, and Protestantism is filled with deadness and is without Christ. It preaches and teaches Christ in name, but it does not have Christ in actuality.

BEING SAVED FROM THIS CROOKED GENERATION, THE PRESENT EVIL AGE

We must all realize that on the earth today there are four negative items: Judaism, Catholicism, Protestantism, and worldliness. The first three are in the category of religion. Today's generation, particularly in the United States, is filled, composed, and constituted with worldliness plus Judaism, Catholicism, and Protestantism. A capable, young man in America may love his car, education, house, job, wife, and family. Moreover, he may attend a synagogue of Satan, a cathedral of demons, or a Protestant church that is dead. Such a person needs to take the word that Peter spoke on the day of Pentecost, "Be saved from this crooked generation" (Acts 2:40). According to the context of Acts 2, it was the Jewish religion with its leaders, priests, and elders that crucified the Lord Jesus (vv. 22-23, 36). This was the crooked generation that they were a part of. Now they needed to save themselves out of this generation. This simply means that they should give up their religion and come to Christ and the church. As Peter was standing there speaking to the people, the glorious church was there, and the Jewish religion as the crooked generation also was there. Those people needed to make a decision concerning their destiny, whether they would remain in the crooked, religious generation or come to the straight, glorious church life.

Paul also told the churches in Galatia that Christ died on the cross for their sins not to bring them into heaven but to rescue them out of the present evil age (Gal. 1:4). What bothered and frustrated the churches in Galatia at that time was the evil age composed with two elements, the Gentile world and the Jewish religion. Today the principle is the same. The evil age in the United States is composed of four elements: worldliness, Judaism, Catholicism, and Protestantism. Even many of the free groups today are a damage to the building up of God's testimony. Thus, they also are a part of today's crooked generation, from which we need to be saved.

Today there are only two things on the earth: the crooked generation and the testimony of Jesus. When Peter stood on the day of Pentecost, the crooked generation was the Jewish religion, and the testimony of Jesus was the church. Likewise, when Paul wrote the letter to the Galatian churches, the present evil age was the Gentile world plus the Jewish religion, and the testimony of Jesus was the church. Today the crooked generation is modern worldliness plus Judaism, Catholicism, and Protestantism, and the testimony of Jesus is still the church. Whoever is not in the church as the testimony of Jesus today is in the crooked generation. Whether someone goes to the casinos in Las Vegas, a Jewish synagogue, a Catholic cathedral, a Protestant chapel, or a meeting place for a free group, as long as he is not built up in the church, he is in the crooked generation.

We look to the Lord that He would grant us a full revelation of the testimony of Jesus. We must never be drugged by worldliness, Judaism, Catholicism, and Protestantism. The satanic, demonic, devilish generation today is composed with not only the casinos in Las Vegas but also with the cathedrals, sanctuaries, chapels, and meeting places of many divisive, dissenting groups. As long as someone is not in the church, he is not in the testimony of Jesus. Rather, he is in the generation of today's crooked world. May all the veils be taken away from us, and may we have a clear sky concerning the testimony of Jesus.

Satan and the demons are very subtle, so we must be careful. We have seen some dear ones seduced and deceived by Satan to speak critically of the church. We must be warned. For over forty years I have never seen anyone who opposed or criticized the church receive God's blessing. If the recovery of the churches is something of the Lord in His governmental way, we must be careful about touching it. It is not a small thing to touch the church. If this is my work, your work, or the work of a movement called "the local churches," we can reject it without opposing the Lord Jesus, but if this is the Lord's governmental move, His economical administration, we must be careful. Some have condemned us, saying that we are heretical. If they were right, they should have received the blessing from God. However, they did not receive the blessing. Time will vindicate who is under God's blessing and who is not. We must be saved from today's crooked and perverse generation—from modern worldliness and from Judaism, Catholicism, and Protestantism. Then we must come to the church as the testimony of Jesus today. Hallelujah, we are here for the testimony of Jesus! This is not a gospel-preaching work, a mission work, a Bible-teaching work, or a work merely to edify Christians. This is the testimony of Jesus. May the Lord open our eyes, and may the heavens be open to us in these days.

CHAPTER SEVEN

OVERCOMING THE PRESENT EVIL AGE BY THE ENJOYMENT OF CHRIST IN OUR SPIRIT

Scripture Reading: Rev. 2:7, 17; 3:12-13, 20-22; 12:1-5, 10-11, 17; Phil. 2:12-13, 15-16a

The church as the testimony of Jesus is a testimony against this evil generation. God's eternal purpose is to have a corporate expression of Himself. For this purpose, He created man in His own image (Gen. 1:26). However, man failed God in this matter, but the Lord Jesus came as the second man (1 Cor. 15:45, 47), who was successful in expressing God. Therefore, Jesus is the testimony of God, signified by the golden lampstand in Exodus 25:31-40. Now Jesus as the unique lampstand is spreading Himself, branching out, as signified by the six branches of the lampstand. The one lampstand has become seven lampstands (Rev. 1:12, 20). The one testimony has become a sevenfold corporate testimony and expression of God Himself.

BEING SAVED FROM THE CROOKED AND PERVERTED GENERATION

Satan always comes in to damage what God does. God created man in order to have a corporate testimony of Himself. This was something wonderful, but Satan, the serpent, quickly came in to damage man, and the man whom God created to be His testimony fell again and again. By the time of Noah, mankind had fallen to such an extent that it became a crooked generation contrary to God. The Lord Jesus likened the present age to the days of Noah (Matt. 24:37-39). In the New Testament this present age is called a crooked and perverted generation (Phil. 2:15), and when Peter stood up on the day of Pentecost, he told the people, "Be saved from this crooked generation" (Acts 2:40). When man's nature was changed into that of a crooked and perverted generation, God's judgment came in. Under this judgment, God revealed to Noah the way for him to be saved out of that perverted generation, instructing him to build an ark, which would save him through water not only from God's judgment on the earth but also out of that perverted generation (Gen. 6:11-14; 1 Pet. 3:20). The water of the flood executed God's judgment upon the entire world, and it also separated Noah from the crooked and perverted generation. Moreover, the ark ushered Noah and his descendants into a new age on a new earth, where they began a new generation. Noah and his family living on the new earth was a type, a shadow, of the church life today.

Not long after that, however, Noah's descendants were divided into the nations, from which Babel was raised up (Gen. 10:32; 11:9). This forced God to call Abraham out of that situation (12:1-2). However, even Abraham's descendants fell into Egypt, where there was another perverted generation. Therefore, God came in again to call Abraham's descendants and bring them out of Egypt (Exo. 1:1, 13; 3:8). This exodus was not only out from God's judgment but, even more, out from the Egyptian generation. The water of the Red Sea executed God's judgment on Pharaoh and all his army, and the water also saved Israel out of Egypt and the evil power of Pharaoh (14:27-30). Noah was saved through water out of his generation, and Israel was also saved out of Egypt through the water of the Red Sea.

After the Israelites were delivered out of the Egyptian generation, God charged them to build a tabernacle, which was the testimony of God against the present evil generation in Egypt (25:8-9). Then after they fought to enter into the good land, they built a temple as the testimony of God against the nations, who were the crooked and perverted generation at that time (2 Sam. 7:12-13; 1 Kings 6:1). Among this crooked and perverted generation there was the temple as God's testimony on the earth. Nevertheless, Satan came in to also damage that testimony, not only by outward destruction but also by inward corruption. The Babylonian army came to destroy the temple outwardly, and after the Jews returned from Babylon and rebuilt the temple, Satan corrupted the divine worship inwardly, changing the testimony of God into the system of Judaism. Therefore, even Judaism became a crooked and perverted generation.

JESUS COMING AS THE TESTIMONY OF GOD, TESTIFYING TO THE EVIL GENERATION OF JUDAISM

Eventually, the Lord Jesus came as the testimony of God, not only against the Roman Empire but also against the present generation of the Jews, Judaism with the temple. The temple was built to be God's testimony against the Gentile nations, but that temple was inwardly corrupted by Satan and changed into a corrupted system that became a sinful, evil generation. The Lord Jesus came to be the living testimony of God, testifying mainly against that system. When the Lord Jesus came, the very God whom the Jewish religion worshipped came. However, He was opposed and persecuted by Judaism, which claimed to worship God. One day this God, who was Jesus Himself, went into a small house at Bethany to talk with Mary and Lazarus and be served by Martha (John 12:1-3). Jesus, as God Himself, was happy there. While He was talking, fellowshipping, drinking, eating, and rejoicing with those dear ones, the priests with all the Jews were worshipping God in a very orderly and seemingly scriptural way. However, at that time God was not in the temple; He was in that small house at Bethany. This did not seem to be according to the Scriptures. The Old Testament did not seem to tell people that God would be in a small "cottage." Nevertheless, this is what Jesus did.

Today it is easy to know the history of the Gospels, but at that time if we had been seeking after God, we probably would have gone to the temple, not that small house. However, if we had gone to the temple, we would have missed the mark. God was not there. We would have needed to go to that small house in Bethany to worship God in a simple way, not with an altar, rituals, or a priest in priest's robes. Eventually, it was the chief priests, elders, and scribes who condemned to death Jesus, who was God. They stirred up the people to shout, "Crucify Him" (Mark 15:11-13), and in this way they killed the very Savior who was their God.

THE CHURCH BEING THE TESTIMONY OF JESUS, TESTIFYING AGAINST THE CROOKED GENERATION

On the day of Pentecost Peter condemned the Jews, saying, "This man, delivered up by the determined counsel and foreknowledge of God, you, through the hands of lawless men, nailed to a cross and killed; whom God has raised up...Let all the house of Israel know assuredly that God has made Him both Lord and Christ, this Jesus whom you have crucified" This word pricked their heart, and they asked, "What should we do, brothers?" (Acts 2:23-24a, 36-37). Peter did not tell them to be saved from hell to go to heaven. The gospel he preached was, "Be saved from this crooked generation" (v. 40), which was the Jewish religion that had killed Jesus. As a result, three thousand were saved, not only from hell but also from that evil generation. Then all these saved ones remained together, loving one another, and they became the church, the testimony of Jesus against the crooked generation.

THE LOCAL CHURCHES BEING THE LORD'S RECOVERY, TESTIFYING AGAINST THE EVIL GENERATION OF CHRISTIANITY

The church is the testimony of Jesus protesting against the crooked, evil, perverted generation. However, even the church as the testimony of Jesus became corrupted. Satan corrupted the testimony of God in the Old Testament time and changed it into the system of Judaism. Then in principle, he did the same thing with the church. Eventually, out of the church as the testimony of Jesus, Satan created Catholicism, another crooked and perverted generation. Later, at the time of Martin Luther, God raised up the Reformation to separate His people out of the Catholic Church, calling His people out of the perverted generation of that day (Rev. 18:4). Once again the ones whom God saved became the testimony of Jesus. Again, though, various doctrines came in to divide Christians firstly into the state churches, such as the Church of England and the Church of Denmark, and then into the private churches, such as the Lutheran, Baptist, Episcopalian, Presbyterian, and Methodist Churches. Today we also have the charismatic movement, with the Lutheran charismatics and the Catholic charismatics. This confusion and division has become another "ism," Protestantism. Today people often ask what kind of Christians we are, whether we are Catholic, Episcopalian, Presbyterian, Methodist, Lutheran, or something else. This question indicates that Christianity has become a crooked and perverted generation.

The generation today is composed of four things: worldliness, Judaism, Catholicism, and Protestantism. Therefore, the Lord says, "Come out of her, My people" (Rev. 18:4). We are standing here as the testimony of Jesus against this present crooked and perverted generation composed of these four items. We are no longer Lutherans, Presbyterians, Episcopalians, or Methodists. We are the local churches outside of worldliness, Judaism, Catholicism, and Protestantism. We are standing on the ground of the church, testifying against this crooked generation. Based on the history of Christianity, some may be concerned that one day even the local churches will be corrupted by Satan. However, I believe that the Lord will come back before Satan can corrupt the local churches. This old age will be terminated, and we will usher in the kingdom age. We are bold to say this, because according to the Bible, the recovery of the local churches as the testimony of Jesus is the final recovery in this age. The local churches are precious, dear, and prevailing. This is not man's work. This is the Lord's recovery of His testimony today on the earth. Whoever does not take the way of the churches will miss the mark of God's work.

The world situation today indicates that the time for the Lord's coming is near. The re-formation of the nation of Israel has been accomplished, and Jerusalem has been returned to the Jews. Only one thing, according to the prophecy of the Bible, remains to be accomplished outwardly, which is the building of the temple on the proper site in Jerusalem. The nation of Israel today is waiting for this, and we are praying for it. The situation in the Middle East is setting the stage for the war at Armageddon (16:12-16; 19:11-21). This will be the time for the

Lord Jesus to come to tread the great winepress of the fury of God (14:19) and terminate this age.

OVERCOMING THE PRESENT EVIL AGE BY ENJOYING CHRIST IN OUR SPIRIT

In the seven epistles in Revelation 2 and 3 we can see worldliness (Pergamos, 2:13), Judaism (the synagogue of Satan, v. 9), Catholicism (Jezebel, v. 20), and Protestantism (Sardis, 3:1). Under these circumstances, Christ calls us to overcome. We must overcome worldliness, Judaism, Catholicism, and Protestantism by eating Jesus. Verse 7 of chapter 2 says, "To him who overcomes, to him I will give to eat of the tree of life." Eating Jesus is the way. We need to forsake all the Jewish rituals, Catholic ordinances, Protestant practices, and worldliness. The only thing we need to do is to eat Jesus. We should say, "O Lord Jesus, I do not care for all those other matters. I only care for eating You." We are no longer under the Jewish rituals, the Catholic ordinances, the Protestant practices, or the influence of the Christian free groups. Rather, day by day we are feeding on Jesus. We have no rituals, ordinances, or any practice that we insist upon. Strictly speaking, we are not shouting Christians or silent Christians. We are simply eaters of Jesus.

Christ Being the Life-giving Spirit in Our Spirit

Certain persons oppose us mainly on three points. They do not agree that Christ is the life-giving Spirit, that we need to exercise our spirit by calling on the name of the Lord, or that we are mingled with God by eating Jesus. This is because they do not have these experiences. They have rituals, ordinances, and practices. They may even have speaking in tongues and the manifestations of the so-called gifts. However, they do not know Christ as the life-giving Spirit (1 Cor. 15:45b; 2 Cor. 3:17), they do not know that Christ is now with our spirit (Gal. 6:18; 2 Tim. 4:22), and they do not know how to turn to their spirit and exercise their spirit to contact the Lord and enjoy Him by saying, "O Lord Jesus" (Rom. 10:12-13; 1 Cor. 12:3). Because these things are foreign to them, they condemn us, calling us mystics, which was the name given to some in earlier centuries who sought the inner life.

A certain brother once told me, "Christian teachers in America tell people to look to the Lord in the heavens, but since you have been in this country, you have always told people to turn to their spirit. Your teaching is different from ours." He even suggested that this teaching is "oriental." This is altogether not logical. Our teaching does not come from the Orient; it comes from the New Jerusalem in the heavens. Romans 8:34 tells us that Christ is in the heavens at the right hand of God. However, in the same chapter, verse 10 says that the very Christ who is in the heavens is also in us. Christ is both in the heavens and in us. We may illustrate this with electricity. The same electricity is both in the power plant and in the room we are in. In order to apply the electricity, we do not need to call the power plant far away, pleading, "Please send me electricity." Rather, because the electricity has been installed in our home, we simply need to turn on the switch. When we turn on the switch, we get the electricity. I am a small man sent to tell you, "Do not look to the power plant; simply turn on the switch." Christ as the heavenly "electricity" is in the heavens, and He has also been "installed" in us. Christ is in you, and Christ is in me. We care for the Christ who is in us. When we need Him, it is not necessary to pray to Him as if He were far away in the heavens. This is foolish. The apostle Paul says, "The Lord be with your spirit" (2 Tim. 4:22). Therefore, we all need to turn to our spirit. When we turn to our spirit, calling, "O Lord Jesus," we are in the third heavens. This is the true enjoyment of Jesus.

Christianity has missed the mark of the indwelling Christ. Some even oppose this teaching. Catholicism teaches people to listen to the pope, worship idols, and burn candles, and Protestantism teaches people to keep the traditional, doctrinal teachings. They do not tell people to enjoy the indwelling Christ, who is the life-giving Spirit. In fact, many who oppose us do not even agree that Christ today is the life-giving Spirit. I always point them to 1 Corinthians 15:45b, which says, "The last Adam became a life-giving Spirit," and 2 Corinthians 3:17, which says, "The Lord is the Spirit." If Christ were not the Spirit, how could He be in us? We are not for mere doctrinal teachings, which mean little; we are for the experience of Christ. We have been fighting the battle for the enjoyment of Christ as the Spirit for over twenty years. The reason we are so much for Christ as the Spirit is that in order to experience Him, we must realize who He is and where He is. We know where Christ is and how to experience Him. He is the life-giving Spirit, and He is now in our spirit.

The Fresh and Living Experiences of Christ Being the Enjoyment of the Indwelling Triune God

The objective "fundamentalists" mainly care for doctrines in a traditional way. In the church life, though, we are not for the traditional way. We are for the fresh and living experiences of Christ. We must check everything against the subjective experience of Christ. Some say that the Triune God—the Father, the Son, and the Spirit—are three separate persons. However, we cannot say that there are three persons within us. According to our experience, the Triune God within us is one. Whether we call on Him, saying, "O Lord," or "O Father," He is the same One. When I was young, I was taught that I should address my prayer to the Father, not to the Son or to the Spirit, because the Holy Spirit is only the "working power," and the Son is the means through whom we pray to the Father. Sometimes, though, I became confused. As I prayed to the heavenly Father, I sometimes said, "O Lord." Then I would repent, ask for forgiveness, and begin again to pray to the Father in heaven. Eventually I realized that this is unnecessary. Our experience tells us that the Father is the Lord, and the Lord is the Father (Isa. 9:6; John 14:9-10). We do not need to differentiate the Father from the Lord in our prayer and experience. Many in Christianity simply fight, oppose, and argue according to their traditional teachings without knowing the experience of Christ. Their experience is poor, and their traditional teachings keep others in poverty.

Eating Jesus to Be Transformed and Built Up in the Local Churches

We only know to eat Jesus, and we have the assurance

that the way to eat Jesus is to call on Him, saying, "O Lord Jesus, Amen, Hallelujah!" If we repeat this three times early in the morning, we will be watered. We have seen that Revelation 2:7 speaks of eating the tree of life. Verse 17 says, "To him who overcomes, to him I will give of the hidden manna, and to him I will give a white stone, and upon the stone a new name written, which no one knows except him who receives it." This indicates that if we eat Jesus, we will be transformed. Then verse 12 of chapter 3 says, "He who overcomes, him I will make a pillar in the temple of My God, and he shall by no means go out anymore, and I will write upon him the name of My God and the name of the city of My God, the New Jerusalem, which descends out of heaven from My God, and My new name." If we are the overcomers who eat Jesus, we will be transformed into white stones, and we will be built into the temple. According to Revelation 21:22, the temple will be the city of New Jerusalem itself. There will be no temple in the New Jerusalem, because the temple will be enlarged to be the city itself. Eating Jesus, being transformed, and being built up is our experience in the local churches, and this is the testimony of Jesus against the nations, the denominations, and the crooked, perverted generation.

THE CHURCH AS THE HEAVENLY BRIGHT WOMAN TO BRING FORTH THE MAN-CHILD

The entire book of Revelation unveils the revelation of Christ and the testimony of Jesus, and the testimony of Jesus is simply the local churches. In the first three chapters of this book, the local churches as the testimony of Jesus stand against the present crooked and perverted generation composed of the world, Judaism, Catholicism, and Protestantism. As the testimony of Jesus, we are protesting against these things. Then Revelation 4 through 11 unveils the world situation. We are not in the world, like the church in Pergamos, where Satan's throne is (2:13). After this, chapter 12 unveils a wonderful woman—pure, genuine, bright, and heavenly, shining with the light-bearers, the luminaries, in the universe—the sun, the moon, and the stars. This woman is the totality of God's people, composed especially of the church. In the book of Revelation there are two lines, or categories, of women, each with its own consummation. The first is Jezebel, signifying the Catholic Church, issuing in the great harlot, Babylon the Great (2:20; 17:1-5). The other line is that of the pure woman, who is first the bright, wonderful woman in chapter 12 and eventually the bride of Christ, the New Jerusalem (19:7; 21:2).

Which line are we on? We may be on the line of the bright woman, but some of the old traditions of the old religion may still remain in us. I was on the line of the old religion for many years. I was taught according to the traditional teachings of Christianity, and it took me many years to drop all the wrong things that I learned. In Christianity I learned to speak for the Lord in a formal way. Gradually, though, I realized that this is simply according to the old traditions and ordinances of religion. Today when I speak, I may say, "Praise the Lord, I have something wonderful to tell you!" When David brought the ark to Jerusalem, David rejoiced and danced before Jehovah (2 Sam. 6:12-15). David's wife despised him for that, but her condemnation of him caused her to lose her fruitfulness and be barren (vv. 16, 23). Today we rejoice before the Lord, proclaiming that He is good for food as the tree of life and the hidden manna. If we all eat the Lord Jesus in a joyful way, we will bear much fruit. We are not bound by any ordinances or practices. Today we may be silent, but tomorrow we may come together as the living testimony of Jesus to shout, "Hallelujah, praise the Lord, Amen!" before all the demons on the earth and angels in the air. We care only for eating Jesus. We are not under Catholicism, Judaism, or Protestantism, and we are not in worldliness. We are the heavenly woman.

The woman in Revelation 12 is in the heavenlies, being clothed with the sun and having the moon underneath her feet and a crown of stars on her head (v. 1). We must be bright, having no darkness or hidden motives. Everything must be in the light. We must not be political or two-faced. Some Christians may say one thing to people's face, another thing behind their back, and yet something else on another occasion. We must not do this. The shining woman is sincere, thorough, frank, honest, bright, and pure as crystal. We are not Jezebel; we are a part of the heavenly woman full of light, with the shining sun, moon, and stars. When many of us were in the denominations, everything was opaque to us, but when we came into the church, we came into a clear sky. All around us everything is crystal clear. We can even see clearly into the lake of fire, where John saw Satan and the beast (19:20; 20:10). We were never before as clear as we are now in the church. Many of us can testify that since we came to the church, the light has been shining. This is because the church is the greater part of the shining woman as the testimony of Jesus, testifying against the crooked, evil generation.

By our shining we testify against the hierarchy, division, and confusions in the denominations. Because of this, opposition has come to us. This opposition is not merely against one person; it is against the testimony of Jesus as the bright woman with the shining sun, moon, and stars. The ministry in the Lord's recovery was sent to this country with the Lord's commission, His burden, the pure Word, the shining light, the reality of life, and the newness of the spirit. The opposition cannot prevail against these things. This shining woman will prevail as the New Jerusalem in the new heavens and new earth. Moreover, this shining woman will bring forth the man-child, the stronger ones, the overcomers, who defeat the enemy because of the prevailing blood of the Lamb and the word of their testimony (12:5, 11). Then through the overcomers the kingdom of God and authority of Christ will come. Today we are in this wonderful woman as the testimony of Jesus.

CHAPTER EIGHT

ENTERING INTO THE CHURCH LIFE AS TODAY'S ARK ACCORDING TO THE LORD'S PRESENT REVELATION

Scripture Reading: Gen. 1:26; 7:1, 16; 9:1; Phil. 2:12-15

The purpose of God's salvation is not only that man be saved but also that he would be a testimony of God. The Bible records that all the saved ones throughout the ages were not only for their salvation but for God's testimony. We can see this clearly in the case of Noah. At the time of Noah the generation was degraded, but God came in and called Noah to build an ark (Gen. 6:11-14a; 1 Pet. 3:20). The ark was not only to save Noah from God's judgment and eternal perdition. Even more, it was, on the negative side, to save him out of that degraded, perverted generation, and, on the positive side, to usher him into a new age in order to carry out God's eternal plan, His testimony, on the earth.

From the beginning God's purpose in creating man was to have a corporate expression of Himself. The corporate man was destined to be God's expression. This is why man was made in the "mold" of God's image (Gen. 1:26). Man is a copy of God, and God is the mold in which, through which, by which, and with which man was copied. Moreover, man is a copy of God, not mainly to serve God, work for Him, or worship Him but to express Him. The thought that man is made to worship, serve, and work for God and behave himself for His glory comes from fallen, degraded religion. It sounds nice, but in actuality it is a devilish concept. There is nothing in the beginning of Genesis that tells us that man was made to serve God, worship God, and work for God, or to behave himself for

God's glory. Rather, Genesis says that man was made in the image of God in order to express Him.

God does not want us merely to work for Him. He can work out everything Himself. He can simply call the things not being as being (Rom. 4:17). When He says, "Light," light comes. He can say, "New heaven and new earth," and the new heaven and new earth will be here. There is no need for us to work for Him. We are nothing, and we can do nothing for God. When someone takes a photograph of a person, he has no intention for the photograph to worship him or work for him. In His creation, God took a "photo" of Himself with the intention to glorify Himself. Man was not destined to worship God, serve Him, or work for Him; he was destined to glorify God. To glorify God does not mean that we do something to give Him glory. God does not need us to give Him glory. Rather, He needs us to simply glorify Him, that is, to express Him.

To this end, God may say to us, "The heaven is My throne, and the earth is My footstool. I do not need you to work for Me, and I do not need you to worship Me. I already have millions of angels serving, working, and ministering for me and also worshipping Me. The four living creatures say, 'Holy, holy, holy' day and night without rest. However, neither the heavens, the earth, nor all the angels can express Me. Therefore, I need you not to do anything else but to express Me. You were made in My image; you are My photograph. Do not try to take the angels' job and forget your own function. Your destiny is to express Me." However, for man to be a "photograph" of God cannot in itself adequately and livingly express God. We also need Him to enter into us to be our life, our nature, and our everything. Even if we would lose our temper, we must do it by Him to express Him.

If a photograph would say to the one who took it, "I want to worship you," the person would reply, "How foolish. I do not want you to do that." Then the picture may say, "Dear master, I would like to shine your shoes and wash your shirt." The person may reply, "You can do nothing for me. This is nonsense." After this the photo may say, "Poor me! I am not qualified to worship or to serve you. I am useless and disappointed." We are here with a burden to bring glad tidings to all the "photographs": Do not be disappointed; be encouraged, because you have a higher mission. Your destiny is not to worship God, work for Him, or serve Him. Your destiny is to express Him. All the "photographs" should be joyful and say, "Have you seen the wonderful person whom I express? Hallelujah, now I know my function and my destiny. I am here simply to express Him." This is our heavenly, wonderful function.

I would ask you to read your Bible again. In the first two chapters of Genesis there is nothing that says we must work for God, worship God, and serve Him. This thought, that fits our natural concept, came from Judaism, Catholicism, and Protestantism. Genesis 1 and 2 simply tell us that we are God's image. We are destined eternally to be His image and expression. This expression is the top worship, work, and service to God. God has the heavens for His throne, the earth for His footstool, and millions of angels to serve Him, work for Him, and worship Him. Now God needs a corporate expression to glorify Him. This is the real definition, meaning, and significance of the testimony of Jesus.

In Revelation, the final book of the Bible, the Lord also does not tell us to do something for Him. Instead, the entire book of Revelation shows the need for the testimony of Jesus. Jesus needs us not to worship Him or work for Him but to be His corporate expression. The poor thought of Christianity is too selfish, only considering people's own salvation, welfare, peace, and joy. These things are like "candy" to the listeners. A good mother would never allow her children to eat too much candy and dessert instead of proper, nourishing food. Sweets damage the proper appetite, and they cause children to have a bad temper. This is an illustration of much of today's teaching in Christianity. All the itching ears like to hear comfort, peace, joy, and rest (2 Tim. 4:3). If someone goes to them to say, "You need to be the testimony of Jesus at any cost," they would reject him. They may say, "What do you mean by this? We are saved, and we will go to heaven. Jesus is sweet and good to us. When we have trouble, He rescues us, and if we have suffering, He comforts us. Our pastor has always taught us in this way. Where did you come from? This is your Eastern mystical philosophy." Almost no Christian minister dares to say something against today's trend of Christianity. If he does, his financial support may be cut off. However, those sent by the Lord are never afraid of having their supply cut off. They would give their life for this.

NOAH ENTERING INTO THE ARK TO BE SAVED FROM HIS GENERATION AND USHERED INTO A NEW AGE

As we have pointed out, Noah was saved not only from God's judgment but also from the crooked, perverted, and evil generation. When Noah went into the ark, Jehovah shut the door (Gen. 7:16). It is as if God were saying, "Even if you change your mind, you cannot get out. I have shut you in, and you must stay here." This kind of salvation may have seemed like a prison. In one sense Noah was saved and rescued, but in another sense he was imprisoned. One of his daughters-in-law might have said, "I prefer my old house with many bedrooms, bathrooms, and a large living room. What you preached to us was good, but this ark is like a prison." It is the same in principle today. I have served the Lord for over forty years, and I have suffered many things. A number of times my children came to me and said, "Father, according to your ability and education, we should not have to suffer this much. Other people did not get as much education as you did, and they are not as capable, but now they have nice houses, stores, land, and bank accounts. What do you have? You have only one room, in which the whole family lives. Those who appreciate and respect you live in mansions, but we are in a prison." Noah might have replied to his daughters-in-law, "What can I do, and where can we go? I cannot open the door. It is not up to me; it is up to Jehovah. He shut us in. We simply need to remain here. Do not be bothered; be patient and wait for a little while longer." After the flood, Noah came out of the ark with his whole family and entered into a new age (8:16, 18).

This shows the kind of salvation Noah secured and enjoyed. It was a salvation not merely from eternal perdition but out of the crooked, evil generation and into a new age. However, when Noah came out of the ark, God had no intention to make him a king. God's intention was still that he and all his children would be His corporate expression. Genesis 9:1 says, "God blessed Noah and his sons and said to them, Be fruitful and multiply and fill the earth." Because man was made in God's image, for Noah and his sons to multiply was for them to be a multiplied expression of God. God did not have the intention to make them kings with a good life and many acres of land. Rather, they were to continue God's purpose in creating man to be His image as His corporate expression.

NOT ALL OF GOD'S PEOPLE BEING SAVED FROM THE CROOKED GENERATION AND ENTERING AS KINGS INTO THE NEXT AGE

At Noah's time there must have been more than eight persons who feared God and believed in Him. According to Genesis 5, the early forefathers lived for a long time. Being godly, they taught their second, third, and further generations to fear God and trust in Him. Therefore, we can be assured that besides Noah and his family, there must have been a number of others who believed in God. Although these may have been saved from eternal perdition, they were not saved from their perverted generation, and they were not ushered into the new age. Some may question how it could be that some outside the ark were saved. However, consider the daily life of many who believe in the Lord Jesus, who go to the movies, attend nightclubs, watch television, and follow the modern fashions. Those who partake of these corruptions may be saved from eternal punishment, but they have not been saved from today's crooked generation, and many will not be ushered into the kingdom of Christ to be kings there. No one who has truly been saved from today's crooked generation follows the course of today's present age. On one hand, we are saved because we believe that the Lord shed His blood and died for us. Therefore, we will not perish for eternity. On the other hand, though, we may still go to the department stores to buy the things of the modern, worldly fashions. If the Lord comes tomorrow, are we assured that He will usher us into His kingdom? Rather, we may be punished along with the present generation.

WORKING OUT OUR OWN SALVATION FROM THE CROOKED AND PERVERTED GENERATION

In the Bible there is such a picture of this. Only eight persons were saved in the ark, through water, from that crooked generation. Many may have been saved from eternal perdition, but not many entered into the ark. In order to be saved from eternal perdition, there is no need for us to do anything, but in order to be saved from the evil generation, we need to build up the ark. Philippians 2:12 says, "Work out your own salvation." Fundamentalists may be unhappy with this verse, because they insist that we are saved by faith through grace apart from any work and that it is heresy to say that we are saved by works. However, at least one verse in the New Testament tells us to work out our own salvation. This is not salvation from eternal perdition. It is salvation from the crooked and perverted generation mentioned in verse 15. This verse says, "That you may be blameless and guileless, children of God without blemish in the midst of a crooked and perverted generation, among whom you shine as luminaries in the world." Many of us can only say that we have been saved from eternal perdition. We may have been rejoicing, saying, "Hallelujah, I have been saved! I will never perish. Heaven is mine, and hell is gone." However, we should not overly rejoice. This is only half of our salvation. We also need to be saved from the other half, from this crooked and perverted generation.

To be saved from the crooked generation is not as easy as being saved from eternal perdition. To be saved from eternal perdition requires us simply to say, "O Lord Jesus, I am a sinner. I thank You that You died for me. You are the Son of God, and You are my Savior. Lord Jesus, forgive me. I repent and believe in You." This is sufficient for our salvation by grace. However, the remainder of our salvation requires our cooperation with God. Verse 13 says, "It is God who operates in you both the willing and the working for His good pleasure." To this we need to say, "Amen to Your work." If we cooperate with God's operation, on the negative side, we will spontaneously be rescued out of this crooked generation. On the positive side, we will enter into the ark, which signifies the proper church life.

We need to enter into the proper church life, which is a "prison" to us. Many people are free to go everywhere, seeking sports, entertainments, and sightseeing on their holidays. They are truly out of prison. The church people, however, remain in their "prison." The parents of some of the saints say, "Pity yourself. Do not go to your church so often. You have been going to your church every Saturday and Sunday. That is enough. Do not forget that this is a holiday. Why would you not take a vacation and enjoy yourself?" However, those who speak in this way do not realize that we have something better and higher. They do not know the heavenly, spiritual, and wonderful "entertainment" that we enjoy. We are imprisoned in the church life, and we love it. The church is a prison, but it is also the best "entertainment."

THE CHURCH LIFE BEING THE PLACE WHERE THE BELIEVERS CAN BE SAVED FROM THE EVIL GENERATION

Many at Noah's time may have been saved from eternal perdition, but only eight were rescued from their generation and put into the ark. The church is the place where we can be saved from today's generation. The New Testament tells us that after the Lord's resurrection, He showed Himself to five hundred brothers at one time, but on the day of Pentecost only one hundred twenty were meeting together (1 Cor. 15:6; Acts 1:15). In addition to the five hundred brothers, there may have been many more saved ones. Through the Lord's ministry of three and a half years, many hundreds may have been saved, but on the day of Pentecost only one hundred twenty were present. All the others were saved, but they were not in the "ark." Only the one hundred twenty were in the ark. No doubt, Nicodemus and Joseph, the ones who buried Jesus, were also saved. They were good, but they were not among the one hundred twenty. They were saved, but they were not in the church practically. They should not have been satisfied in that condition. No one should have said, "As long as I am saved, everything is all right. I still prefer to remain in the temple with the altar, the priesthood, and the burning lamps. I realize that this religion put Jesus to death, but I myself believe in Jesus, I love Him, and I am for Him." Nevertheless, regardless of how much many people seemed to be for Jesus, they were not in the church life.

Today many Christians are like this. One person recently told me, "I surely appreciate your ministry. It is wonderful. However, I am a Catholic. I love Jesus, yet I also love Catholicism and all the things in it. In the Catholic Church today there is the charismatic movement, and many people there like to read Watchman Nee's books." In truth, this is a pitiful stand to take. What God wants today is not millions of saved individuals. What He wants is the church, the ark. He wants to save us from the crooked generation and usher us into God's kingdom to fulfill His eternal purpose. He does not care for a charismatic movement or for speaking in tongues. God only cares for whether or not we are in the ark, the proper church life. He wants us to be a part of the testimony of His Son, Jesus.

THE LORD RESERVING A REMNANT TO BE SAVED FROM THE EVIL GENERATION AND TO BUILD UP THE CHURCH LIFE

In the ancient time, all the Israelites were God's people. They worshipped God in the temple, and they read and studied the law of Moses. However, one day Elijah accused them, saying, "The children of Israel have forsaken Your covenant, thrown down Your altars, and slain Your prophets with the sword; and I alone am left, and they seek to take my life." The Lord replied to him, "I have left Myself seven thousand in Israel, all the knees that have not bowed unto Baal and every mouth that has not kissed him" (1 Kings 19:10, 18). Seven thousand is a good number, but compared with millions of Israelites it is small. Today the situation among Christians is the same. All are God's people, but almost all have "bowed unto Baal." Baal was an idol, and the principle of an idol is that it is something besides God that occupies people. The department stores, our improper shopping, our way to spend the money the Lord gives us, long hair, a short skirt, modern fashion, television, and the newspaper may all be idols to which many believers have been bowing and still are bowing. Day by day God's people may be worshipping cars, houses, clothing, education, fame, position, and promotion. Even a certain reverend, pastor, or denomination may be an idol to someone. Those who have idols do not love the Lord at any cost and give up everything else. Whatever we still hold on to is an idol. Apparently not many today love the Lord absolutely, but in actuality the Lord has reserved a certain number for His church life who are building the ark to be saved from today's generation, to save others also, and to have the church life.

THE HIGHEST EXPERIENCE OF SALVATION BEING IN THE LOCAL CHURCHES AS THE GOLDEN LAMPSTANDS

The book of Revelation is not about our personal salvation. It is about the golden lampstands. Many Christians do not care about the lampstands in Revelation. They may feel that the lampstands and the golden city with twelve gates are too mysterious and that it is more practical to tell people the stories of Jesus from Matthew and John, about how He loved Mary and Lazarus and performed miracles. As we have said before, many Christians have been "drugged," caring only for their eternal salvation, even though they may have been saved only to a small degree. People may not like to hear that they have been saved only to a small degree, but eventually everyone will face a situation which will expose how much he has been saved. We can fool man, and we can fool the church, but we can never fool God. The book of Revelation contains the highest salvation, which is the golden lampstands, today's ark, the churches.

OUR NEED TO BE IN THE LOCAL CHURCHES IN PRACTICALITY

Some people question us as to what we mean when we speak of the church, asking, "Do you mean that only you are the church?" We should check again with our Bible. The Lord appeared after His resurrection to five hundred brothers at one time, but only one hundred twenty were in the practical church life. We should not think that as long as we are Christians, we are in the church. If we do, we may deceive ourselves and deceive others also. We may be members of the church in name, but this means little if we are not in the church practically. We may illustrate this with the Jews on the earth today. There are more than twelve million Jews today, and in New York City alone there are about one million. To be sure, all these are genuine Jews. Every one of them can say, "I am a member of the Jewish race." Nevertheless, not all of these Jews are the nation of Israel. In order to be the nation of Israel, they must return to their fathers' land. Some may object to this and say, "Do not be so narrow-minded. How can I go back to Israel? I have my house, my business, and my investments here. Every month I send much money to help Israel." Regardless of how much money anyone sends to help Israel, he is still not in the nation of Israel. He is only a helper to Israel. Only those who go back to their forefathers' land are the nation of Israel today. In the same way, regardless of how good a Christian someone may be, as long as he is not in the local churches, he is not the church practically. He is a member of the Body of Christ, but he is not in the practical church life. To be in the church in practicality, we need to pay the price to come into the local church. This is not a small matter.

When certain missionaries asked me, "Do you mean that you are the church, and we are not?" I replied, "You do not need to ask me. Simply ask yourselves. You call yourself Presbyterians, but if you are Presbyterians, you are not the church. You do not like for us to call ourselves what we are, but if we do not call ourselves the church, what should we call ourselves? If a woman is the wife of Mr. Smith, then she is Mrs. Smith. It is not logical for someone to claim to be Mrs. Smith yet go by the name of Mrs. Johnson." These dear missionaries eventually realized that they could not argue with me. If they did, they would lose their case. However, before they argued with me, they had already lost their case. If they call themselves "Mrs. Johnson," they have no case to claim that they are "Mrs. Smith." Therefore, I told them, "If you want to be the church along with us, get rid of the name Presbyterian." However, they answered that they could not do that. As long as they cannot give up the name Presbyterian, they are not the church in practicality. Instead, they are still in Protestantism, which is a part of today's crooked and perverted generation. The Lord desires only a pure church, a pure golden lampstand, a pure bride. To still keep some mixture is confusion. It is not the church, and it will not be a part of the New Jerusalem. Instead, it will be burned with Babylon.

We must all be saved from the crooked generation by building up the ark. Even while we are speaking these things, we are building. To say that Judaism, Catholicism, and Protestantism are all part of today's generation and that only the local churches are the ark seems very bold. Nevertheless, we must fight for this truth throughout the entire world. We must fight against today's perverted generation, which includes the world, Judaism, Catholicism, and Protestantism, and even the free groups with their speaking in tongues. They are not the church but a part of today's crooked generation.

THE PROPER CHURCH AS THE LORD'S TESTIMONY BEING IN THE UNIQUE FELLOWSHIP OF ALL THE CHURCHES

The Lord desires one church in every locality and one Body in the entire universe. Therefore, no church should say, "Since we are the local church in our city, we want nothing to do with the other churches." Whoever cuts themselves off from the fellowship with all the churches universally is no longer a local church; they have become a local sect. Regardless of how much some claim to meet in the Lord's name according to the teaching of the New Testament, and even according to Brother Watchman Nee's books, if they cut themselves off from the Lord's flow today, they are a local sect. They are not the church but a counterfeit, an imitation. Some have used the messages of my ministry from our tapes and our books, yet they have openly rejected this ministry. Morally speaking, this is not right, and we cannot believe that the Lord will honor this. Are those who do this the church in practicality? To act in this way is not to be the pure woman clothed with the sun, with the moon underneath her feet, and a crown of stars on her head. Instead, it is to be one of the daughters of the great harlot, Babylon (Rev. 12:1; 17:5). It is subtle to steal someone's messages yet reject his ministry. If certain ones do not receive my ministry, they should reject my books and tapes also. They are not right, honest, or moral.

God desires only one church. We cannot see in Revelation more than one woman in the heavens, shining with the sun, the moon, and the stars. There is no doubt that every local church is independent according to its locality, but we also must realize that all the local churches are one Body. Only those who are ambitious, who desire to have a little empire, would say, "We are the local church here, and you are the church in your locality. Do not interfere with us." Yes, we are the church in our locality, but we take the way to fellowship and be one with all the churches; however, others are the local church in the way of cutting themselves off from the flow of the Lord's testimony today. This is not the church the Lord desires today. It is an old antique, in the principle of the practice of Brethrenism. That may have been good a century ago, but it is not good today. What the Lord desires today is the present testimony of Jesus.

TAKING THE WAY OF THE LORD'S UP-TO-DATE REVELATION

In the ancient times, people walked with God in the way they had learned from their forefather Enoch (Gen. 5:22-24). At a certain point, however, Noah was raised up to build an ark. Some might have said to him, "We have never heard of building an ark. Our forefathers instructed us concerning godliness, telling us to take the way of salvation according to Adam, to please God according to Abel, to call on the name of the Lord and enjoy all His riches according to Enosh, and to walk with God according to Enoch. I walked with God for many years before you were born. How can you tell me something new? Did God tell you that a flood will come? Why did He not tell Enoch? This is your own foreign concept." The preaching of Noah did not mean that people should not take Adam's, Abel's, Enosh's, or Enoch's way. However, God had His up-to-date revelation. Merely to be saved—as Adam was—or to please God, call on the name of the Lord, and walk with God—as Abel, Enosh, and Enoch did—would no longer satisfy God. At that time, there was only one thing that could fully satisfy God and rescue people from that crooked generation, and that was to build the ark.

The principle today is the same. Someone may say, "I was born in America. I am sixty-five years old, I have more than one Ph.D., and I know many things in Christianity. I have also read church history and many books from the past centuries. However, I never heard this term *the local church.* Who are you? You are a little Chinese man from the land of the heathen with their philosophical Confucian thought. What can you know? This is your Eastern concept." However, do not argue. Simply wait and let time prove the fact. Those who do not receive this way will one day have to agree that this is God's present revelation. We, the little brothers in China who were raised up by the Lord fifty years ago, do know the way to be saved, to preach the gospel, to call on the Lord's name, and to walk with God. We have practiced these things for many years. However, one day the Lord showed us that all these are not adequate and up to date. There is only one thing the Lord desires today—the local churches as the golden lampstands according to the revelation in the last book of the Bible. Watchman Nee was captured by seeing this, and he truly influenced me. I told him, "This is it! Let us take this way at any cost," and by the Lord's mercy, we did take this way. From that day, more than forty years ago until the present, I have never changed my tone. In the United States I have been ministering for over twelve years and have put out many messages, but from the first day up until today my tone has always been the same. This is not an "Eastern philosophical thought"; it is the divine revelation from the Bible today.

THE LORD HAVING A UNIQUE MEANS FOR HIS REVELATION IN EVERY AGE

Some among us have been accused of following one man. Recently a number of leading brothers all expressed to me that they felt they must follow this ministry. At that time I was burdened to tell them, "To declare that you follow someone is nonsense. It is entirely not a matter of following a man or not following a man. It is altogether a matter of where the present revelation is." If we were born and lived in Noah's age, we would have needed to follow Noah, because he had God's revelation. Apart from Noah, we could not have had the revelation of that age. If someone had said, "I do not follow Noah. I will follow someone else," then he would have missed the mark. If I am speaking for my own sake, I must be stopped, but I am not speaking for myself. I am speaking the truth. Please read your Bible again. In every age, in every generation, there was only one means for the revelation in that age. Noah, Moses, and David were the unique means in their age, and Peter, Paul, and eventually John, in the book of Revelation, became the unique means of God's up-to-date revelation. I strongly declare that when I was with Brother Watchman Nee, I respected him not because he was good but because he was the unique means of God's revelation in that time. In every age God had and still has one unique means for His up-to-date revelation.

A TESTIMONY CONCERNING THE MINISTRY IN THE PRESENT AGE

It was through this ministry that the Lord's recovery was brought to this country, and many have received help from it. Regrettably, though, some have utilized the materials of this ministry to establish a church in their own "pocket." They declare, "We are the local church here," but they are not a genuine local church. Because that church is not open, it is a church not of the saints but of someone's private concern. This is not the church the Lord desires today. It is the church of someone's own work and a church for that work. It is someone's "pocket version" of the church life. In the churches in Los Angeles and Anaheim, we never closed the door to others. Whoever wished to come to us was able to. I would speak a word to the dear ones who keep the churches as their "pocket church": Will you open the door of your church to everyone? If you will, I will be the first to speak an approving word. However, I am afraid such a church will reject this ministry, accusing me of trying to be a "pope" to control them. I have no intention to be the pope, but those who keep this kind of church do have the intention to be a king in their "empire."

I labored closely with Watchman Nee, so he told me things he could not tell others. He suffered much, because some were accusing him, saying, "You are trying to be a pope, using your ministry, your gift, your messages, and your knowledge of the Bible to control all the churches." Brother Nee told me, "Only robbers always suspect others of robbing them. You know that we have no thought of controlling others. They are able to think this way only because they are the 'robbers.' If they were in our position, they would surely be 'popes' to control others. Because they are 'robbers,' they think we are robbing others too." Some have accused me also of trying to set up a "papal system" and of putting out messages to control all the churches. I never had such a concept. How can the dear ones have such a concept? It may be because they are "robbers." If such ones were in my situation, they might set up such a papal system.

Those who have been in the church life for many years can declare to the entire universe that I have controlled nothing. Nevertheless, in every age there is a means for God's up-to-date revelation. The things this ministry is speaking are unique. This ministry today is burdened directly for the Lord's present revelation. If the Lord would not give me something to minister, there is no need to pick up something old from the other books. Those things are out of date. They might have been good one or two centuries ago, or even fifty years ago, but they are not good for the present revelation. Anyone can compare our messages with the other books to see that all the points in our messages are unique. This revelation is from the Lord, not from me. This is why I have the full assurance that if anyone opposes this ministry, he will suffer the loss of the Lord's revelation today.

I am forced by the present situation to speak in such a way in order to warn you not to listen to and be poisoned by critical and divisive speakings that damage our one accord. We have no intention to control anyone, and we are not qualified to control anyone. According to their natural thought, some believe that I control the church in my locality. In 1965, the brother helping me to file my income tax asked me if I knew how much money had been given to me in the previous year by the church in my locality. When I told him that I do not pay attention to such things, he told me the amount, which was a very small figure. This illustrates that this ministry has no intention of controlling anyone. This ministry cares only to minister the Lord's burden in His present revelation.

Some saints have been listening to my messages for many years. Many of them considered that eventually I would have no more new messages and that I would simply repeat my old ones. However, throughout all the years, our conferences have never been a mere repetition. There is always something new. This is due to the Lord's mercy and grace, because this is not my ministry but His. Since 1950, every time I visited Manila the brothers there have asked me to hold a conference, and every time the Lord has given me something new. One elderly sister testified that she was surprised when I came with new messages. She said, "I am a third generation Christian, but I have never heard the terms you spoke in your message. Please tell me where you found these new things." I told her, "After coming here for so many years, you should have realized where I receive my messages. I do not get them from a seminary or merely from bookshelves or a reference Bible. I receive my messages from only one source—the One on the throne that flows out the living water."

THERE BEING ONE FLOW FROM THE THRONE AND ONE SOUNDING OF THE TRUMPET

In the entire universe there is only one flow, but whether anyone follows the messages from this flow is up to him. I have declared this for many years. The first message I published in the first issue of *The Stream,* on July 1, 1963, was entitled "The Divine Stream," concerning the one flow on this earth. This was the reason that I chose the name of the magazine. The stream is the unique flow from the throne. In the entire universe there is only one flow. We can see this in the Acts. After the day of Pentecost the one flow flowed from Jerusalem to Antioch, and from Antioch the flow turned to Europe. Since Barnabas had brought Paul into the Lord's ministry, he may have thought that he could dissent against him (Acts 15:39). However, after he separated from Paul, there is no further record in Acts concerning his work. This is because he left the one flow.

I am forced to speak concerning my ministry in this way, not for my sake but for the sake of the churches. Whoever rejects this ministry rejects not a small man from China but the flow from the throne. This ministry has only one burden, which is to build today's ark, not only to save the saints from God's eternal judgment but also to save them from the crooked and perverted generation of today so that they may express God in a corporate way, be ushered into the coming kingdom, and exercise His authority in the kingship. This is the purpose, the burden, and the goal of this ministry as God's unique means for His revelation. God would not send out trumpeters to sound different trumpets for His army to fight the battle (1 Cor. 14:8; Num. 10:9; Judg. 7:18). This would be confusion. God is wiser than this. He will raise up only one trumpeter to sound one calling, one voice, so that His people on the earth can march on.

Chapter Nine

EIGHT ASPECTS OF THE TESTIMONY OF JESUS

Scripture Reading: Rev. 1:11-13, 20; 7:9-17; 12:1-2, 5-6, 9-11; 14:1-5, 14-16; 15:2-4; 19:7-10, 14-20; 17:14; 21:11, 18-19; 4:3a; 14:8; 17:1-5; 18:2a, 4; 19:1-6

THE SHINING GOLDEN LAMPSTANDS

The book of Revelation reveals eight aspects of the church as the testimony of Jesus. The first aspect, in chapters 1 through 3, is the seven golden lampstands. The lampstands themselves have three main significances. First, the lampstands shine in the dark night. Second, the lampstands are golden. In typology, gold signifies the divine nature. Everything in the church as the testimony of Jesus must be in the divine nature. Third, the shining of the golden lampstands is so that people may see Christ as the Son of Man walking in their midst. If anyone says, "You talk so much about Jesus, but where is He?", we can boldly point them to the churches. We can answer, "Come and see Jesus in the churches." Today Jesus is walking, acting, moving, living, working, and saving people in the local churches. The present age is the "nighttime," and in every corner and avenue of human society there is nothing but darkness. However, every local church is a shining lampstand, illuminating people that they may see Christ. When people see Christ in the churches, they can realize that the churches are not low, mean, earthly, sinful, or mixed. Rather, everything in them is golden and divine. This is the first aspect that Revelation reveals to us concerning the churches as the testimony of Jesus.

All the golden lampstands are identical to one another. Many Christians, having taken in a mistaken concept, desire to be different from other Christians. When I came to this country fourteen years ago, I met some dear Christians who were troubled because the local churches were all the same. They told me that they preferred to be different. This is not right. We may compare the identical nature of the lampstands to the similarities of our physical bodies. Since everyone is created with the same organs, it would be foolish for anyone to say that he wants a different number of organs in order to not be the same as others. Those who claim that every local church should be unique base their concept upon the differences among the seven churches in Revelation 2 and 3. When I was young, I was influenced by this concept and I taught the same thing. However, one day the light dawned upon me, and I saw that all the differences in the local churches in Revelation 2 and 3 are negative, not positive. Ephesus lost her first love (2:4), Pergamos is worldly (v. 13), Thyatira is demonic (vv. 20, 24), and Laodicea is lukewarm (3:15); all these are negative matters. On the positive side, however, all the local churches are identical, because they all are golden. If we were to place the seven lampstands before us, we would not be able to tell them apart. All the seven lampstands are the same.

Nevertheless, some people in this country have boldly declared that they will never be like the other churches. However, many of these voices have now faded away, and the peculiar concepts they advocated have failed. It is not that we must all follow one certain church. Rather, it is that we all must have the same "number of organs," that is, the same nature and appearance. On the positive side, all the local churches must be identical, but on the negative side, they are different. If one church begins to worship idols, we must refuse to follow that church. In matters such as this, we must be "different." However, it is wrong to say that the local churches should not be the same in the positive matters. We should not try to make ourselves peculiar or different; this is to be proud. The four sides of the New Jerusalem are all built with the same material—jasper (21:12-14, 18). It is not that one side is built with jasper, and another side with a different material. Because we are all one church universally, the local churches throughout the earth should be identical, not in every practical matter but in nature and appearance. Locally, we are the churches; universally, we are the church. This is the testimony of Jesus.

A GREAT MULTITUDE OF THE REDEEMED SAINTS

In 7:9-17 we see the testimony of Jesus as a great multitude, those who have been redeemed "out of every nation and all tribes and peoples and tongues" throughout all the generations. Verse 14 says, "These are those who come out of the great tribulation." This refers to the tribulations, sufferings, persecutions, and afflictions experienced by God's redeemed people throughout the ages. Because the world always afflicts the church (John 16:33), wherever the church is, there will always be a certain amount of persecution. This great multitude has come out of tribulation in a victorious way, for they all hold palm branches, which signify their victory over tribulation. Revelation 7:15 says, "He who sits upon the throne will tabernacle over them." Eventually, in eternity, God will overshadow them with Himself as their tabernacle (21:3; cf. John 1:14). This is the destiny of God's redeemed ones. How wonderful this is! Furthermore, the Lamb will also shepherd them and guide them to springs of waters of life for eternity (Rev. 7:17).

Verses 9 through 17 do not portray any particular group of believers. Rather, they present a general record of the whole of God's redeemed ones and their state in eternity. In eternity, their state will be that of enjoying God's overshadowing and Christ's shepherding. This is our destiny. This portion of the Word reveals that while Christ is executing God's judgment upon mankind, He will take care of God's redeemed ones. All God's redeemed ones eventually will be raptured to the throne of God and will stand there enjoying God's overshadowing and the Lamb's shepherding.

THE UNIVERSAL, HEAVENLY, AND BRIGHT WOMAN

Following this, chapter 12 reveals the third aspect of the testimony of Jesus. Here the figure is not a lampstand but a wonderful, universal, heavenly woman (vv. 1-2, 5-6). Whereas the lampstands are in the dark night, the woman is full of light. With her there is no distinction between day and night, because she is clothed with the sun, the moon is underneath her feet, and on her head is a crown of stars. There is no need for the woman to shine in the darkness, as the lampstands do, because she is always fully in the light. When we come to the lampstands, we are under the shining, and when we come to the woman, we are under the sun, the moon, and the stars.

The sun, the moon, and the stars are all heavenly (Gen. 1:16-17). Thus, the woman indicates the heavenly nature, position, and disposition of the church as the testimony of Jesus. With her there is nothing earthly, such as casinos, department stores, television, sports, synagogues, cathedrals, or chapels. Everything about this woman is heavenly. Some gatherings of Christians can be compared to a dark cell deep in the earth, having no openings for the light and being full of dirt. When they meet together, they talk about fashions, department stores, and worldly places. The local churches, however, are in the heavens. There is no earth but only the sun, the moon, and the stars. The earthly dirt is under our feet.

Christians today sometimes speak about fighting Satan. However, as long as someone is in that dark "cell" of the world, he can never fight against the devil. He is good only to be Satan's food. When God cursed Satan as the serpent, He condemned him to eat dust (3:14). As long as we are earthly, we are qualified to be food for Satan. However, there is no serpent on the sun, the moon, or the stars. The position of the church in the spiritual warfare is not on the earth but in the heavenlies (Eph. 2:6; 6:12). When the church is in the heavenlies, Satan is under her feet. Eventually, Satan is cast down and defeated by the man-child of the wonderful heavenly woman (Rev. 12:10-11). In earthly Christian meetings, people are good for Satan's food, but in the proper church life, which is the main part of the heavenly woman, Satan is already defeated. The best way to defeat Satan in the local churches is to minister the heavenly things to the saints so that the church may remain heavenly. Then there will be the victory, and Satan will be cast down.

According to our observation, the weakest point with the sisters is gossiping. Many young sisters like to gossip about their mothers-in-law, and many older sisters like to gossip about their daughters and daughters-in-law, about who is engaged, married, or pregnant, when the baby will come, and whether it will be a boy or a girl. Such gossip belongs in worldly places, not in the local churches. Gossiping causes the church to be dark and opaque. Whenever the long gossiping tongue is "cut off," the church is in the heavens. Many times the love that some of the saints have is a fleshly love, not the love in the spirit that is as clear as crystal. This kind of ugly, fleshly love causes many Christian meetings to be darkened. In the eyes of the Lord, it may be worse than hatred and fighting. It is the love of "turtles" and "serpents," and it should be buried and burned. Likewise, the more people are humble in a natural way, the more they sink into darkness. Again, in the Lord's eyes, soulish humility may be worse than pride. A sister may say, "I dare not speak. I am just a little sister. What can I say? I am not worthy," but this is only a soulish humility. Because the church is heavenly and crystal clear, we should all be frank in a heavenly way, taking no excuse or cloak, but being what we are in the Lord and in the Body. To cloak ourselves is to pretend to be something that we are not. The heavenly woman wears no cloak. The church is crystal clear and frank, having no pretense, excuse, cloak, or covering. With her, everything is in the open.

Nice words are often a cloak. Many times, certain dear saints came to me to speak nice words. Right away my spirit told me, "This is a falsehood, and these nice words are a cheating." We should not deal in this way with the church life. Nothing exposes people as much as the church. The church life is the strongest "x-ray." Someone may come to us speaking good things, but if we are in the spirit, the "x-ray" within may see the workings of their mind and that those words are a cheating. Several times I told someone, "Please do not come to cheat me. I hear your words, but my spirit sees what is in your heart." If the church is heavenly, everything will be in the open. The wonderful, bright woman has no covering, shadow, or darkness. Everything is in the bright open air. This kind of church is a victorious one. In this sense, there is no need for the church to fight against Satan; Satan is already defeated and cast down, and the kingdom of Christ is brought in. This woman is heavenly, bright, frank, and thoroughly crystal clear. It is from such a wonderful church that the man-child is brought forth (v. 5a). This woman is the third aspect of the church as the testimony of Jesus.

THE MAN-CHILD

The man-child is the stronger part of the people of God. Among the people of God, even among those in the Lord's recovery today, there is the stronger part. The woman will be left on earth to pass through the great tribulation, but the stronger part, the man-child, will be raptured to the throne of God before the tribulation (vv. 5b-6). The man-child will be raptured prior to the tribulation because God needs the man-child to fight against Satan in the heavens and cast him down to the earth (v. 9). Although God has many angels who will fight against Satan, the final victory over the enemy will be gained not because of the angels but because of the man-child. God needs the man-child. God will shame Satan by using the very man Satan corrupted to defeat him. God may say, "Satan, you have corrupted the man I created, but I have produced a man-child out of this corrupted man to defeat you, not only on the earth but also in heaven." The man-child will fight up to the throne to cast Satan down from the heavens to the earth. Although Jesus has defeated Satan on the cross, there is still the need for the church to execute His victory over the enemy. Because many members of the Body have failed in this matter, only the stronger part of the Body, the man-child, will execute Christ's victory over Satan. The man-child will be raptured to the heavens to accomplish this job.

The rapture is not mainly for our own blessing. We should not merely say, "How good it is for me to be raptured to the heavens!" We must realize that God has a need for us to be raptured; we must be raptured to heaven to fight against the enemy. If someone hears this and says, "I don't want to go to the heavens and be involved in a war," this means that he is not qualified to be raptured before the tribulation. If anyone does not go to heaven to meet Satan and cast him down, Satan will come down to the earth to meet and overcome him.

We must be the man-child. I earnestly desire to be a part of the man-child. I am not satisfied simply to be a part of the woman. I want to be included in that stronger part. This also is an aspect of the testimony of Jesus.

A FARM TO GROW THE FIRSTFRUITS AND THE HARVEST

The fourth aspect of the church as the testimony of Jesus is that it is God's farm to grow the divine crop. This crop is first the one hundred forty-four thousand firstfruits, a small number, and then the harvest, the majority (14:1-5, 14-16). This tells us that in the church life we all need to grow. Verse 4 shows the way to grow. This verse says concerning the firstfruits, "These are they who have not been defiled with women, for they are virgins. These are they who follow the Lamb wherever He may go." In order to grow, we need to stay away from any kind of defilement. Daniel and his three friends were offered the best food by the royal palace in Babylon, but Daniel purposed in his heart not to defile himself by eating food that had been offered to idols. In this way, these young men kept themselves from being defiled (Dan. 1:5-6, 8). Everywhere on the earth today there is defilement. Young people especially must be careful not to be defiled, and they must also follow Jesus wherever He goes. If the young people will follow Christ, they will not go to casinos, because Jesus never goes there. If the young people will do this and separate themselves to the Lord, they will grow every day, and they will be the firstfruits produced by the church life.

When I was in Christianity, I did not observe much growth there. People can sit in Christian meetings for many years and still remain the same. This is because Christianity is not a farm but an "iceberg" on which nothing can grow. The Sunday morning service is a time mainly for people to relax in the pews. In speaking this I am defaming no one; I am simply speaking the truth. If we mean business in the church life, we will grow week after week. Recently a certain brother was captured by the Lord after visiting the homes of the saints. At that time, he had a long beard, but we said nothing to him about it. However, after a short time in the church he received some transformation, and he shaved his beard. Another young brother with his wife were among us, continually enjoying the Lord, but for over a year he also had a beard. In the church we do not have any ordinances. Our only "ordinance" is that we should not regulate anyone. Because of this, we stopped ourselves from saying anything to him about his beard. Recently, though, I saw that he had shaved his beard. His wife said, "I have a 'new' husband." I told him, "To be sure, you are another person." Later he testified that he had kept his beard because he thought that to deal with it was too religious. Nevertheless, the anointing within him bothered him and required him to shave it off. We can tell many stories like this. In the local church the crop is growing.

If we simply come to the church meetings and follow the flow to say, "O Lord, Amen, Hallelujah!" we can be assured that we are growing and that we will not remain the same. We thank the Lord that we are especially seeing the young people growing in the church life. It is not adequate to say that we are the church. What kind of church are we? If we do not see the young people in the church growing, this indicates that the church in our locality is not fertile soil. The church must be fertile, and we must all be growing in life.

THE OVERCOMERS ON THE GLASSY SEA

The Glassy Sea Indicating the Principle of Baptism

Revelation 15:2-5 reveals the fifth aspect of the testimony of Jesus—the overcomers standing on a glassy sea mingled with fire before God's heavenly temple. A number of the saints are on the shore of this sea, singing the song of Moses and the song of the Lamb. This is a picture signifying further spiritual matters concerning the testimony of Jesus. The church as the testimony of Jesus is composed of a group of saints who have been saved through water, just as Noah was saved from his evil generation through the water that flooded the earth (Gen. 6:11-14a) and as the Israelites were saved through the water of the Red Sea not only from God's judgment but also from the evil power of Pharaoh (Exo. 14:22, 29).

The final chorus of *Hymns,* #438 says, "I've crossed the Red Sea of His death, / And left the world behind me." The flood for Noah and the Red Sea for the Israelites were both a baptism (1 Pet. 3:20-21; 1 Cor. 10:1-2). Today we, the New Testament believers, are also baptized. The real meaning of baptism is that it is a burial (Rom. 6:4). A certain man may be a millionaire with banks, corporations, and many friends and relatives. It will certainly be hard for such a man to break all these ties, but on the day he is buried, he will finally come out of the world. Nothing separates us from all the worldly ties as thoroughly as burial. Anyone who means business with the Lord must see that he has come out of the world by passing through water. The water of the Red Sea will never allow us to return to Egypt.

Moreover, in front of the tabernacle there was the laver (Exo. 30:17-21). The laver did not wash away sins; it was the altar that did this. However, even after passing through the altar, people still could not come into the presence of the Lord without passing through the laver to wash away the dirt of worldliness. This also signifies baptism. After the Israelites entered into the good land, they built the temple. In front of the temple was a bronze sea with ten bronze lavers (1 Kings 7:23-40a), the fullest type of baptism. The first event that transpired in the New Testament was baptism. John the Baptist called people to repent, and he baptized those who came to him (Mark 1:4; Matt. 3:5-6). This was to terminate people, bury them, and take them out of this world. All the believers must pass through a genuine baptism. In principle, the glassy sea before the throne of God signifies the operation of baptism. Eventually, in Revelation 15 certain of the saved ones are standing on the shore of "baptism," rejoicing and singing just as Israel sang the song of Moses on the shore of the Red Sea.

The Glassy Sea Being Mingled with Fire, Leading to the Lake of Fire

Revelation 15:2 tells us that the glassy sea is mingled with fire. This sea is not of water but of fire. God's judgment over His fallen creation was firstly with water, but after the flood

God told Noah that He would not judge the earth again with water (Gen. 9:15). Instead, from that time onward God's judgment has always been with fire (19:24; Rev. 14:10; 18:8; 19:20; 20:9-10; 21:8). Therefore, the glassy sea mingled with fire signifies both kinds of judgment by God, that by water and that by fire. This glassy sea eventually issues in the lake of fire. In front of the tabernacle was the laver, in front of the temple was the bronze sea with ten lavers, and in front of the heavenly temple there is the glassy sea. Eventually, outside the New Jerusalem there will be the lake of fire where all the things we buried in our baptism will go. This is our experience in the church. We must put all the dirt of the earth into the "sea" and bury it there.

Experiencing the Glassy Sea in the Church Life

The Israelites were baptized in the Red Sea, but because they had become old and fleshly in the wilderness, they needed to be baptized again in the Jordan. Likewise, we may have been baptized ten years ago, but today we may be full of dirt and old things. We must not bear these things in the church life. In the church there is a glassy sea into which we can jump and be washed. Today the baptistery is an entry for the negative things to go into the lake of fire. We need to let the dirt, the world, and all the negative things pass through that entrance and go into the lake of fire. If we are wearing the modern fashions from the department store, we need the experience of entering into the baptistery to be washed and allow those fashions to go to the lake of fire. Then we will be in the New Jerusalem in our experience. We must not despise the baptistery. It is the best place to send our earthly dirt on the way to the lake of fire. We may also compare the baptistery to the post office. If we feel that we still have some earthly dirt, we should go to the baptistery and "mail" it to the lake of fire. We need to be cleansed, through the entrance to the lake of fire. We must not keep the dirt on ourselves. We must be cleansed in the church.

I do not care for doctrine; I care for real experiences. I have seen many who went into baptism come out rejoicing, like those who will rejoice on the shore of the glassy sea. What a joy it is when all our dirt goes into the baptistery! I am not passing on an official teaching of rebaptism. I do not care for formal teachings. Rather, in principle, I would like to see many saints on the shore of the glassy sea. We wish to see some declaring that the modern fashions they purchased from the department store, that occupied them for many years, are now all gone. This is much better than mere doctrine. This is the principle of the overcomers in Revelation 15. In principle, we too can stand, rejoice, and sing on the shore of the glassy sea today. However, those who have not yet "jumped into that sea" are not able to rejoice. Only when we come out from that sea can we have such joy. This is the fifth aspect of the church as the testimony of Jesus in Revelation. The book of Revelation is truly a wonderful book, and today it is open and crystal clear to us.

THE BRIDE CLOTHED IN FINE LINEN, BRIGHT AND CLEAN

The sixth aspect is in chapter 19, where we see the bride prepared for a wedding by being clothed with fine linen, bright and clean (vv. 7-8). The outer court of the tabernacle was also covered with fine linen (Exo. 26:1). Linen signifies the expression of Christ in the righteousnesses of the saints. Today as the testimony of Jesus the church must be clothed with fine linen, being righteous, bright, pure, clean, clear, and without mixture, spot, or any such thing (Eph. 5:26-27).

The bride will be the church in the millennium, the thousand-year kingdom. Not all Christians will be a part of this bride. Rather, only those who are truly in the church expressing Christ as the fine linen will be there. We should not say that as long as we are in the local churches we will be there. We must be the local churches, but we also must express Christ as our fine linen. Then we will be prepared and qualified to be the bride on the wedding day of Christ. The thousand years will be a wedding day, since with the Lord, one day is like a thousand years (2 Pet. 3:8). On her wedding day, a woman is a bride, but on the next day she becomes a wife. In the thousand years all the overcoming saints will be the bride and will enjoy the wedding feast. However, those who do not express Christ as the fine linen will not be ready, and they will have no share in the wedding feast. Do not ask, "Are they not saved?" Yes, they are saved, but because they have no share in expressing Christ, they will also have no share in that wedding day.

THE OVERCOMING ARMY TO FIGHT AGAINST ANTICHRIST

The seventh aspect of the testimony of Jesus is the overcoming army to fight against Antichrist. The stronger part of the church, the man-child who fights against Satan in the heavens, will also be a part of the army that fights with Christ against Satan on the earth (Rev. 19:14-19). Christ's heavenly army will be composed of all the overcomers, those who are called, chosen, and faithful (17:14). After all the raptured saints are judged at the judgment seat of Christ (2 Cor. 5:10), the overcomers will return to the earth with Christ as His heavenly army to fight against Antichrist with his earthly armies. The false Christ will be so bold as to fight against the true Christ, but the true Christ will war against the false one. Eventually, at the end of this war, Christ will defeat Antichrist (Rev. 19:20).

THE NEW JERUSALEM, HAVING THE APPEARANCE OF GOD AS THE FULFILLMENT OF GOD'S PURPOSE FOR MAN

The eighth aspect of the testimony of Jesus is the New Jerusalem. The wall of the New Jerusalem is built with jasper (21:11, 18-19). When we look at the bride, we see fine linen as the expression of Christ, and when we look at the holy city, we see jasper. The appearance of God on the throne is like jasper (4:3a). Therefore, jasper signifies the precious and divine appearance, likeness, expression, and image of God. That the New Jerusalem has the appearance of jasper signifies that it is the fulfillment of Genesis 1:26. Man was made in God's image to express God, and in the New Jerusalem this purpose will be fulfilled. The entire redeemed human race will express God. The appearance of God is like jasper, and the New Jerusalem will appear the same. Because the New Jerusalem is the expression of God, it will be His consummate, corporate testimony.

In this message we have seen the church in the eight aspects of the testimony of Jesus. Besides this, Revelation also shows another woman, the great harlot, Babylon, that is full of abominations and fornication (17:1-5; 18:2a, 4). Babylon signifies religion plus the world, the present generation, with its politics, diplomacy, and worldly affairs. The church is seen in the lampstands, the great multitude of the redeemed, the shining woman, the growing farm, the overcomers on the glassy sea, the bride clothed with Christ, the overcoming army, and the New Jerusalem with the appearance of God. As such, the church protests against the present generation. Opposite to the church, there is religion—including Judaism, Catholicism, and Protestantism—and the world with its politics and worldly affairs. On one side is the church, and on the other side is the present generation. In order to be on the side of the church, we must be golden and heavenly, we need to grow, and we need to stand on the shore singing and rejoicing that we have been rescued from the other shore. We were on the other shore, but we have been baptized onto this shore; we were in Egypt, but we have been baptized through the Red Sea. Now we are singing the song of Moses and the song of the Lamb. On this side we are expressing Christ as our fine linen, and eventually we will be the New Jerusalem. Moreover, on this side we are protesting against religion, politics, and worldly affairs. On which side are we? Hallelujah, we are on the side of the church as the testimony of Jesus!

This is not something from our own mentality. It is from the book of Revelation. We need a vision to see what is in this book. Revelation has been here for hundreds of years, but people have not seen what is in it. They have not had the vision, but today in the church we have a "skylight," a heavenly opening for the light (Gen. 6:16a). I myself never before saw some of the points covered in this message. Only while I was speaking did I become clear about them, and the more I speak, the more I have something further to speak. To be sure, our eyes and ears have been much blessed. Hallelujah, for the Lord's present, up-to-date revelation concerning the church as the testimony of Jesus! Now we all need to follow this vision.

CHAPTER TEN

THE PRACTICAL WAY TO BE THE TESTIMONY OF JESUS AS HIS FULL EXPRESSION IN THE CHURCH

Scripture Reading: Rev. 1:1-2, 12-16; 5:5-6; 19:15; 2:2, 4, 7, 17; 3:12, 20; 2:9; 3:9; 2:20; Matt. 13:33; Rev. 17:1-5; 3:1, 15-16; 2:13-15

The Bible has a wonderful beginning in Genesis and a wonderful conclusion in Revelation. Without the book of Genesis, the divine revelation would not have a proper beginning. The first ten chapters of Genesis require more than thirty messages of the *Life-study of Genesis* to cover them. Likewise, without the book of Revelation, the Bible would not have a proper conclusion. It is very meaningful that the Bible concludes in the same way it begins. It begins with the tree of life in Genesis 2:9. Then throughout most of the remainder of the Bible, the tree of life seems to disappear. When I read the Bible as a young man, I wondered where the tree of life went after the way to it was closed. Eventually, the tree of life returns in the book of Revelation (2:7; 22:2). In this way, the Bible begins with the tree of life, and it also concludes with the tree of life.

The Bible also begins with man as God's expression (Gen. 1:26). That man was created by God in His own image means that he was created to express God. Man was destined to be the expression of God. In the final two chapters of the Bible, man eventually becomes the true expression of God. The One sitting on the throne has the appearance of jasper, and the New Jerusalem, with man as a component, also has the appearance of jasper (Rev. 4:3a; 21:11, 18-19). That jasper is the appearance of the holy city signifies that man becomes the expression of God. Therefore, in the first two chapters of the Bible there is life and the expression of God, and in the last two chapters there is again life and the expression of God. The only difference is that the Bible begins with creation, but it concludes with building. What is there in the first two chapters of the Bible is mainly God's creation. In the beginning God created the heavens, the earth, and many other items, including man. In the final two chapters, however, there is a city built with precious materials. A city is not something of creation but something that has been built. The building with which the entire Bible concludes is a building with the divine life, and the purpose of the building is to express God. If we grasp these few points, we can see the intrinsic significance of the entire Bible. Therefore, we must spend adequate time to get into Genesis and Revelation.

REVELATION BEING THE UNVEILING OF CHRIST IN A FURTHER, DIFFERENT WAY

The book of Revelation is a mysterious book. On the one hand, it is a book of prophecy, but to say this with the proper understanding requires us to know what prophecy is. Prophecy is not merely a prediction, as the Old Testament prophets would say, "Thus says Jehovah." It is something more weighty, higher, deeper, and more excellent. Although Revelation is a book of prophecy, prophecy itself is not the subject of this book. Revelation 1:1 begins, "The revelation of Jesus Christ." We must keep this in our memory. This is a book of revelation, but the revelation is of Jesus Christ. Among the Christian teachers, there are different schools concerning the meaning of this one phrase *the revelation of Jesus Christ.* Some say this refers to the revelation given by Christ, but this is an inadequate interpretation. This book is the revelation concerning Christ and unveiling Christ.

We may have seen Christ in the four Gospels, the Acts, and all the Epistles, but Christ is much more even than this. Regrettably, most Christians only know Christ mainly from the Gospels and a little from the Acts and the Epistles. In the past fifty years I have met many Christians of different kinds and from different parts of the world, and I have always tried to humbly receive what they had. Throughout my entire Christian life, however, Brother Watchman Nee was the only person I met whose ministry I could fully respect. Among all the other Christian teachers I met, almost no one else truly knew the Christ in the last book of the Bible.

The Christ in Revelation is absolutely different from the One in the four Gospels. In the past I have been condemned for saying this. One preacher even said, "This is heresy. This man says that he has a different Christ." Nevertheless, in this message I repeat strongly, the Christ in Revelation is different from the Christ in the four Gospels. Yes, He is the same Christ, but He is the same Christ in different aspects. In the four Gospels Christ was mild, gentle, and kind. Whenever He looked at people, they felt loved. His most intimate disciple could even recline on His bosom (John 13:23). This same Christ, however, appears differently in the book of Revelation. He has not only two eyes but seven eyes, which are like a flame of fire (1:14; 5:6). If such a Christ appeared to us today, we would all be shocked. Luke 4:22 says that words of grace proceeded out of His mouth, but Revelation tells us that a two-edged sword proceeds out of His mouth (1:16; 19:15). Moreover, in John 1:29 He is introduced as the Lamb of God, but in Revelation 5:5 He is called the Lion of the tribe of Judah. It is foolish to say that the Lion is the same as the Lamb. The book of Revelation unveils Christ to us not in a common way but in an extraordinary way. This way is absolutely different from that in the Gospels. In this sense, Revelation continues the Gospels and the Epistles, but it does not reveal Christ according to the Gospels and the Epistles. The revelation of Christ unveils Christ in a different aspect.

REVELATION UNVEILING THE TESTIMONY OF JESUS

Revelation 1:2 speaks of "the word of God and the testimony of Jesus." For many years I have considered this term *the testimony of Jesus.* When I was young, I was taught that if we have good behavior, we will present the testimony of Jesus to people. This means that we, the believers, must behave ourselves, love our neighbor, honor our parents, love our wife, and submit to our husband. At that time I accepted this definition, but gradually I began to feel that it is too low. Such a definition does not belong in the concluding book of the Bible. Whatever is in the conclusion of the Bible must be something higher. After this, I began to look to the Lord for the way to understand the testimony of Jesus. Gradually I saw the proper meaning, but for over twelve years I have realized that if I spoke about this matter in an honest and frank way, I would offend many people. Twelve years ago the time was not ripe to speak in this way, even in the Lord's recovery, so the Lord caused me to be patient and wait until another day. Recently, however, the burden came to me that now is the time for the Lord to tell His people clearly and fully what the testimony of Jesus is. For this reason I am bold. I do not care if I am rejected. I must speak the truth concerning the testimony of Jesus.

We all know that a picture is better than a thousand words. For this reason, Revelation has not only plain words, but even more it paints a picture. If we do not know how to understand this "painting," we will not be able to understand this book. The first picture is the vision of the seven shining, golden lampstands (1:12). Then in chapter 4 there are the four living creatures; one is like a lion, the second like a calf, the third having the face of a man, and the fourth like a flying eagle (vv. 6-9). In the midst of the four living creatures is One who was introduced as the Lion, but when John looked, the Lion became a Lamb (5:5-6). The third vision is of four horses running a race (6:1-8), a white horse, a red horse, a black horse, and a pale horse. In chapter 9 there are locusts with tails like scorpions (vv. 3, 10). In chapter 12 there is a wonderful woman clothed with the sun, with the moon underneath her feet, and on her head a crown of twelve stars (v. 1). The woman is about to deliver a child, and before her is a great dragon who tries to devour her child (v. 4). Then in chapter 13 are two beasts, one coming out of the sea and the other coming out the earth (vv. 1, 11), and in chapter 16 there are frogs (v. 13); frogs always come out when the weather is bad. In chapter 17 there is not a wonderful, universal woman but a great harlot (vv. 1-6), and in chapter 18 there is a great, evil city that is condemned by God (vv. 2-5). In chapter 19 there is a clean, neat, bright, white, and pure bride (vv. 7-8), clothed in fine linen, with whom there is no mixture, dirt, or spot. Then in chapter 20 there is the ancient serpent (v. 2), and in chapters 21 and 22 there is the holy city, the New Jerusalem (21:2, 9-27; 22:1-2). What marvelous pictures these are! We need to see all these pictures, vision after vision. However, the main, central figure in this whole "painting" is Christ as the Lion of the tribe of Judah. If we see all the other items but not this Lion, we will certainly miss the mark. We must turn our eyes away from the frogs, the beasts, the locusts, the dragon, and the serpent and turn our eyes upon this Lion. This book is the revelation, the unveiling, of this Lion.

THE TESTIMONY OF JESUS BEING HIS FULL EXPRESSION IN THE LOCAL CHURCHES

Moreover, this Lion is expressed through some vessels, which are the testimony of Jesus. An expression is the full testimony of a certain person. The testimony of Jesus is the expression of Jesus, who is expressed first in the local churches today and eventually in the New Jerusalem in the millennium and in eternity. Therefore, the churches today are the testimony of Jesus.

God created man in His own image with the intention that man may express Him. We must all realize that our destiny is not to do certain things. We need to forget about all other things. Our destiny is to express God. In Genesis, after God created man, He did not tell man to do many things. This is because man was made in the image of God simply to express God. We may compare man as the expression of God to a photograph. A photograph of a person does not worship the person, work for him, or serve him. The destiny of a photograph is simply to express the person. Man is a "photograph" of God. When God created man, He "took a photo" of Himself. Just as the function of a photograph is to express a person, man was made to express God. However, many failed God in this very respect, but Psalm 8 tells us that a second man would come to resume the responsibility of man to express God (vv. 4-6). This is what Jesus accomplished. While Jesus was on this earth, He fully expressed God. He was the real "photograph" of God.

Now this one photograph has been reproduced. We are all the reproduced "photographs" of Jesus. Therefore, today God has a corporate expression—the church—which is the testimony of Jesus, who is the expression of God. The old man Adam was created in God's image, but Adam failed God. Now the church is the new man, which is created in Christ according to the image of God, having Christ as God's expression (Eph. 4:24; Col. 3:10). This expression is the testimony of Jesus, which in Revelation is first the local churches and eventually the New Jerusalem. The book of Revelation opens with the seven lampstands, and it concludes with the New Jerusalem. Both the lampstands and the New Jerusalem are figures of the church. The seven lampstands are signs of the seven local churches, and the one New Jerusalem is the sign of the ultimate consummation of the church for eternity. Revelation is an unveiling of Christ, and Christ is expressed through the church. Therefore, the church is the testimony of the very Jesus revealed in this book.

THE PRACTICAL WAY TO BE THE TESTIMONY OF JESUS

The church is a corporate expression of God in Christ. In the seven epistles that the Lord spoke to the seven churches, we can find some secrets of how we can be the expression of God. The Christ revealed in Revelation 1 through 3 is a wonderful person. It is difficult to describe this wonderful person, but we know that in this universe there is such a wonderful One. These chapters first present a vision of Christ as the Son of Man walking in the midst of the seven lampstands, the local churches (1:13; 2:1). Some Christian teachers say that since the lampstands must be in heaven, Jesus is walking among them in heaven. However, since the seven lampstands signify the seven local churches, they are still on the earth. We cannot say that Jesus is walking in heaven among the churches. Verse 11 of chapter 1 says, "What you see write in a scroll and send it to the seven churches." John was not writing to the heavens or to the angels. Instead, he was writing to seven cities on the earth—Ephesus, Smyrna, Pergamos, Thyatira,

Sardis, Philadelphia, and Laodicea. Christ today as the wonderful person is walking on the earth in the midst of His local churches.

To Love the Lord with Our First Love

In this portion of the Word, this wonderful person does not charge us to worship Him, and there is only a small indication that we need to work for Him. The first church, the church in Ephesus, did many good works for Him. Christ appreciated this, but not very much. Mainly, He was not happy with Ephesus. He said, "I know your works...But I have one thing against you, that you have left your first love" (2:2, 4). The first secret to being the church as the testimony of Jesus is that we must love Him. We must say, "O Lord Jesus, I love You. Lord Jesus, nothing is as sweet to me as You are. Lord, I love You sweetly, intimately, and privately. In my love for You, I have many secrets with You that even my spouse does not know of." Can we say this to the Lord? We must have a private love toward the Lord that we have not told even to our spouse. We all need to tell Jesus that we love Him.

To Eat the Lord as the Tree of Life, the Hidden Manna, and the Feast to Be Transformed for God's Building

After this, we also need to partake of the Lord by eating Him. We should not care as much about worshipping or serving Jesus. Strictly speaking, He does not need us to serve Him. He has countless angels to serve Him. Rather, He needs some eaters. He wants us to eat Him (John 6:57). Even if the angels desired to eat Jesus, they do not have this privilege. However, we, His simple followers, do have the privilege. We must know nothing but eating Jesus. Eating Jesus is the way. Revelation 2:7 says, "To him who overcomes, to him I will give to eat of the tree of life, which is in the Paradise of God." If we love the Lord, we need to eat Him. We need to take Him into us as our enjoyment. Nothing is as enjoyable as eating. We can forget every kind of sport and give up all entertainment, but we cannot give up eating. My residence is near Disneyland, but I have never gone there. The best land is not Disneyland but Christ our land. Christ not only gives us the good land; He is the good land. He is our enjoyment, our entertainment, our sport, our amusement, our joy, and our rejoicing. We all need to enjoy Him. To be the proper church is to enjoy Christ, love Him, and eat Him as the tree of life and the hidden manna (v. 17).

Loving Jesus is the first secret, and eating Him is the second. We need to eat Him in both an open way and a hidden way. We can eat Him by pray-reading His word with some other saints (Jer. 15:16). This is to eat the tree of life. However, we also must learn how to eat Him in a hidden way as the hidden manna. It is when we eat Him as the hidden manna that we are given a "white stone"; that is, we are transformed into precious stones, which are for God's building. First we eat Him openly, and then we eat Him in a hidden way to be transformed into stone. Verse 12 of Revelation 3 indicates that the stones are built into the temple as a main part, a supporting pillar, of God's building. Here is an advancement. Verse 7 of chapter 2 speaks of eating, verse 17 indicates transformation into a white stone, and 3:12 speaks of a pillar built into God's temple, which eventually consummates in the holy city. We are being built into the church, which today is the temple and in the future will be enlarged to be the city.

Verse 20 says, "If anyone hears My voice and opens the door, then I will come in to him and dine with him and he with Me." In Greek, *dine* denotes taking the principal meal of the day at evening. To dine is to eat not merely one kind of food but the riches of a feast. This may refer to the eating of the rich produce of the good land of Canaan by the children of Israel (Josh. 5:10-12). The tree of life, the manna, and the produce of the good land are all types of the various aspects of Christ as food to us. We must eat Christ not only as the tree of life and the hidden manna but also as a feast full of His riches.

I would encourage all the young brothers and sisters to take heed to this word. Fifty years ago, when I was your age, I prayed every morning, "Lord, I give myself to You again. I put myself into Your hand. Lord, You must do something for Yourself in this age through this young man." How I thank the Lord that He has answered my prayer. I do hope and expect that from today on, many of the young people will pray, "Lord, help me to eat You as the tree of life and even as the hidden manna in a hidden way that I may be transformed into a white stone to be built into Your temple as a supporting pillar." The Lord's recovery today, particularly in this country, needs many supporting pillars in every place. To this end, we need to pray. I can assure you and testify that this kind of prayer will be fully answered by the Lord.

Now we can see what the church is. The church is the transformed humanity who loves Christ, eats Christ, enjoys Christ, and is transformed by the holy, divine element of Christ into something solid—a white stone for God's building. In one sense, the church is still humanity, but in another sense, it is a stone, a solid, supporting pillar, and a pure, solid, golden lampstand. All these matters are covered in the seven epistles in Revelation 2 and 3.

To Forsake Religion and the World

In the seven epistles to the churches, there are also negative matters. On the one hand, the churches as the lampstands of Christ are the testimony of Jesus. On the other hand, God's enemy never sleeps. We all need to realize that Satan is very busy. Our God also works very diligently, but He is never too busy. He never says, "This morning I do not have time to be with you. Please wait until evening." Rather, whenever we call on Him, He is ready to answer us. However, since the time that the church came into existence, Satan has been constantly busy, doing many things to corrupt and transmute the church and even to change its nature.

Judaism Being Satanic

In the seven epistles, the Lord used very hard and strong terms. He indicated that the Jewish synagogues were no longer of God but the synagogue of Satan (2:9; 3:9). Some may be offended and say, "You are too much. In the synagogue the Jews read the Bible and worship God. How can you say that they are the synagogue of Satan?" However, we must be fair. This is not my word; it is the word of the Lord Jesus. The Lord

Jesus indicated that although the synagogues apparently were something for God, in actuality they had all become something of Satan. Today the principle is the same. Today on the whole earth, all the Jewish synagogues are satanic, and the satanic Judaism is versus the church. Nowhere is the opposition to Jesus so strong as in the Jewish synagogues. Some among us are brothers of Hebrew descent, but they must all realize that the religion of their fathers has become something satanic in the eyes of God.

The Lord mentioned the synagogue of Satan twice, once to Smyrna and once to Philadelphia. This is because among the seven churches, these two were the most positive ones. When the church becomes dull, dark, and down, there is no need for opposition from the synagogues. The synagogues would not care about such a church, because it is so low. However, when the churches become bright and shining, the synagogues hate them. If the churches in the Lord's recovery in the United States become bright, eventually even Judaism will rise up against them. Judaism today is satanic.

Catholicism Being Demonic

After speaking of Judaism, the seven epistles also deal with the Roman Catholic Church. In the eyes of the Lord, Catholicism is Jezebel, the evil woman (2:20), that is not only satanic but also demonic. Judaism is satanic, but it never teaches people to worship idols. In Catholicism, however, Jezebel teaches people to worship idols, which are related to demons. Jezebel is the woman prophesied by the Lord Jesus in Matthew 13:33 and the great harlot in Revelation 17:1-5, the religious part of Babylon the Great. As such, she is a sign, a symbol, of Catholicism. As I mentioned in a previous chapter, when I was in Manila, I went to the largest cathedral purposely to study the situation. I observed all the idols there. Under one idol was a sign saying that if someone prays at that idol a certain number of times a day for a certain period of time, they would reduce a relative's time in purgatory. Of course, they did not call those things idols. They called them Saint Teresa or the "holy mother." The outstretched hand of the statue of the "holy mother" was made of marble, but it was almost worn out, because for many years superstitious worshippers had come and touched it. What superstition this is! This is an abomination in the eyes of God. It is more than satanic; this is demonic Catholicism. This is spoken of in the fourth epistle, the epistle to Thyatira.

In satanic Judaism, the name of God is preached, and people are taught to worship God. Likewise, in Catholicism people are taught about God, Christ, the Bible, and the cross. This is a subtlety. In the parable in Matthew 13, the Lord Jesus said that this woman, Jezebel, took leaven and hid it in three measures of fine flour. Fine flour is pure, but leaven is dirty and evil. This signifies that Catholicism has mixed the "fine flour," the things concerning Christ, with every kind of heathen thing. Opposing the pure church there is satanic Judaism and also demonic Catholicism.

Protestantism Being Dead and Christless

The next item related to religion is Protestantism. Whereas Judaism is satanic and Catholicism is demonic, Protestantism is dead and Christless. We know this from the fifth epistle, to the church in Sardis. Sardis has a name that it is living, yet it is dead (Rev. 3:1). In principle, we also see the condition of Protestantism in the epistle to Laodicea. The Lord told the church in Laodicea that it is neither cold nor hot, and because of this He is about to spew it out of His mouth. Christ is not in such a situation; therefore, He is outside of it, knocking at the door (vv. 15-16, 20). Again, all these things can be seen in the seven epistles in Revelation 2 and 3. Have you seen satanic Judaism, demonic Catholicism, and dead and Christless Protestantism in these epistles? Where then are you?

The World Being the Place of Satan's Throne

The fourth negative factor in these epistles is the world. According to church history, the church in Pergamos was fully married to the world. The Lord told Pergamos, "I know where you dwell, where Satan's throne is...where Satan dwells" (2:13). The world is the place where Satan dwells and where his throne is. Therefore, four negative matters are covered in these seven epistles. The Lord's intention here is to show us the things that are versus the church, His testimony—Judaism, Catholicism, Protestantism, and the world.

The Teachings of Balaam and of the Nicolaitans Damaging the Church

Within Catholicism and Protestantism there are the subordinate items, such as the teaching of Balaam and the teaching of the Nicolaitans (vv. 14-15). The teaching of Balaam was to lead God's people to eat idol sacrifices and to commit fornication, and the teaching of the Nicolaitans was to set up the clergy-laity system. (Please see footnote 1 of verse 6 and footnote 1 of verse 15 in the Recovery Version of the Bible.) Both of these are versus the church life. The church as the testimony of Jesus must forsake satanic Judaism, demonic Catholicism, dead and Christless Protestantism, devilish worldliness, the teaching of Balaam, and the teaching of the Nicolaitans. We are here as the pure golden lampstands.

Chapter Eleven

A FURTHER WORD CONCERNING THE WAY TO BE THE TESTIMONY OF JESUS

Scripture Reading: Rev. 1:11-13, 20; 7:9-17; 12:1-5, 17; 14:1-5, 14-16; 15:2-4; 19:7-10, 14-20; 21:1-3, 9-11, 18-19

In the previous chapter we saw that Judaism is satanic, Catholicism is demonic, Protestantism is dead and Christless, and the world is devilish. After hearing this, some may consider that this word is hard and without mercy. This is the reason that I have not released such a message in the United States for over twelve years. If I had spoken such a message ten years ago, even some among us would not have been able to receive it. However, now is the time to release this word. We are not the first ones to speak in this way, apparently without mercy. It was the Lord Jesus who pointed out these diabolic matters in His seven epistles to the churches in Revelation 2 and 3, and we are simply His small followers. In these seven epistles, the Lord Jesus used the term *synagogue of Satan* twice (2:9; 3:9). Then in speaking to the church in Thyatira, He mentioned Jezebel. Jezebel was an evil woman in the Old Testament during the time of the kings, but now the church in Thyatira tolerates that evil woman (2:20). According to church history, Thyatira symbolizes the Roman Catholic Church. In the eyes of the Lord, the Roman Catholic Church has become Jezebel, the evil woman who teaches God's people to commit fornication and to worship idols. Thus, in the fourth epistle the Lord used the words *Jezebel, fornication,* and *idol sacrifice,* and He also mentioned the "deep things of Satan" (v. 24), the mysteries of Satan taught not only in the idol temples but also in the cathedrals and sanctuaries of the Catholic Church. Therefore, no one should say that we are merciless. The Lord Jesus Himself pointed out the diabolic things in Catholicism.

The Lord told the church in Sardis, "You have a name that you are living, and yet you are dead" (3:1). According to church history again, Sardis signifies the Protestant church, which in the eyes of the Lord is dead and lifeless. Finally, to the last church, the church in Laodicea, the Lord said, "Because you are lukewarm and neither hot nor cold, I am about to spew you out of My mouth." Moreover, He is standing outside the door of the church (vv. 16, 20). This is not our own word. It is the word of the faithful and true Witness (1:5; 3:14). This Witness of God pointed out all these negative matters in the churches. By the Lord's simple and clear word, we can see the real situation in the typical religions, even in the so-called Christian churches. There are the synagogue of Satan, Jezebel, idols, fornication, and the deep things of Satan. Even Protestantism is dead, lifeless, and Christless. Christ has given it up, and He is outside of it. This is the word spoken by the Lord in the Bible.

In addition, the third church, the church in Pergamos, dwelled where Satan's throne and dwelling place are (2:13). The church was not in the place of God's ruling but where Satan's throne is. This place is the world. Today's Christianity is not only devilish but also worldly. Today certain Christian churches even use rock music, drama performances, and dancing as entertainment to draw crowds. This is worldly and is altogether abominable in the eyes of God. Nevertheless, many good Christians justify these things. Almost no one stands up to protest against them. Some have told me, "Brother Lee, you are too old. You are not up to date. You need to know the trend of the world. If we are so straight and old, the young people will not come. We need to fit into the young people's trend." Some even proposed to me that we should form a "hippie church," saying that this would be the best way to follow the tide of the age. This is worldly and diabolic. Christianity today has drugged people with things such as music and dancing. Regrettably, these "drugs" have damaged many Christians in their sober mind that was created by God. Their mental sky is altogether cloudy, and they cannot discern right from wrong. Therefore, when we stand up to protest against these things, they say that we are merciless and unkind, that we should love people and not condemn them. The Lord Jesus loves everyone, but He does not love the things of Satan, such as devilish entertainment.

Satan is subtle. He not only uses these "drugs" to damage the understanding of God's people, but he also uses good things, that we may compare to dessert and candy. Even in fundamental Christianity, we can hear good, sound, fundamental, and scriptural messages, but many of them are merely "sweets" to comfort people and show love to them. Those who are considered to be the best ministers and speakers in today's Christianity are the ones who soothe, comfort, and give rest to their listeners. If anyone is faithful to stand up and tell people that they need the experience of the cross, the listeners will reject him and cut off his financial supply. If we could check with the heart and conscience of certain fundamental preachers, we would find that they do know what the Lord's will is, yet they dare not to preach it. Rather, they pick up many good messages along the line of *Streams in the Desert*. As we said in a previous message, many things in this devotional book are like a "British biscuit" or an "American dessert" that can damage the appetite for proper, solid, and nourishing meat.

Over twenty-five years ago, when I came out of mainland China, I received the burden to preach concerning the New Jerusalem. The Lord had shown me that the New Jerusalem is not the "heavenly mansion" of the so-called heaven but a living composition of all God's redeemed ones. I preached this, and I taught it strongly. Then a certain preacher in Hong Kong rose up to tell people, "Brother Lee is taking away the heavenly mansions from the believers." He asked me, "If you take away the heavenly mansions from the believers, what will we tell them when their relatives die?" I told him, "You are deceiving people with your superstition, telling them that their parents are in the heavenly mansions where you say we will all go one day. Do you really believe this? Do you not know that this is the superstition of Buddhism that was adopted by Catholicism? Have you not read in Revelation 21:2

that the New Jerusalem will come down out of heaven? The mutual abode of God and man for eternity will not be heaven but the New Jerusalem on the new earth. The teaching that you use to comfort people is a superstition, even a lie." However, most people prefer to listen to the lie. They do not like to listen to the truth. The New Testament is full of solid food (Heb. 5:13-14; 1 Cor. 3:2), but in the Catholic Church and also in the Protestant churches, no one dares to touch this solid truth for fear of not being accepted even by the real, fundamental Christians.

Those in the charismatic movement emphasize nothing but the gifts, and by *gifts* they mainly mean speaking in tongues. However, 1 Corinthians 12:8-10 mentions nine gifts. The two chief items of the manifestation of the gifts are the word of wisdom and the word of knowledge, and the last two are speaking in tongues and interpretation of tongues. To emphasize speaking in tongues is to make the tail into the head. We would rather keep the head as the head. In every meeting we have many words of wisdom and of knowledge. According to the context of 1 Corinthians, the word of wisdom is the word concerning Christ as the deeper things of God, predestined by God to be our portion (1:24, 30; 2:6-10), and the word of knowledge is the word that imparts a general knowledge of things concerning God and the Lord (8:1-7). The word of wisdom is mainly out of our spirit through revelation; the word of knowledge is mainly out of our understanding through teaching. Both of these, not speaking in tongues or any other miraculous gift, are listed as the first gifts and the topmost manifestation of the Spirit because both are the most profitable ministries, or services, for the edification of the saints and the building up of the church to carry out God's operation. According to history, the Christian churches have almost never had so much of the word of wisdom and of knowledge as we have today week after week and meeting after meeting. However, the charismatic movement cares mainly for the "tail." Of course, it is good to keep the tail, but we must not make the tail into the head.

Some have also practiced prophesying by saying, "Thus saith the Lord," but what they predicted was never fulfilled.

Twice in 1963 and 1964 some prophesied that Los Angeles would fall into the ocean, and this was even published in a major newspaper. However, it never happened. Those who practiced in this way were all "drugged." They never saw the fulfillment of their grand prophecies, but they still clung to the gifts. This is a kind of addiction. It is difficult for anyone today to rise up and speak something according to the solid truth, but in the United States today there is a people among whom the solid truth can be released. We thank the Lord for this. I have no intention to condemn anyone. Rather, our burden is to see what the Lord desires to have today. We must go on more and more in a positive way. We should not remain in satanic Judaism, in degraded Christianity—including demonic Catholicism and lifeless and Christless Protestantism—or in devilish worldliness. Whoever wants to remain there, let them remain. We need to go on from all these negative things to the one positive item, the testimony of Jesus.

EIGHT ASPECTS OF THE TESTIMONY OF JESUS IN REVELATION

As we have seen, the testimony of Jesus is the church as the expression, testimony, and revelation of Jesus in a corporate way. In order to see Jesus, we must see Him in the church, because Jesus is expressed and revealed in the proper church life. As we have also seen, because the book of Revelation unveils Christ, in this sense it also is the testimony of Jesus (1:1-2; 19:10). In no other book is Jesus revealed as much in His corporate expression. This book presents eight aspects concerning the testimony of Jesus, in chapters 1, 7, 12, 14, 15, 19, and 21. We should all remember these seven chapters. Chapter 1 unveils the seven golden lampstands (vv. 11-13, 20) shining in the dark night, and chapter 7 shows us the multitude of the redeemed saints in eternity (vv. 9-17). Chapter 12 reveals a wonderful, universal woman with a man-child (vv. 1-5, 17), and chapter 14 reveals the firstfruits and the harvest (vv. 1-5, 14-16), which are grown on God's field, His farm. In chapter 15 we see a group of overcomers standing on the glassy sea rejoicing, praising, and singing the song of Moses and the song of the Lamb (vv. 2-4). In chapter 19 there is the bride on the wedding day (vv. 7-8) and the army of Christ to defeat Antichrist (vv. 14-21), and in chapter 21 there is the New Jerusalem as the wife in eternity (vv. 1-3, 9-11, 18-19). In brief, these seven chapters reveal the lampstands, the great multitude, the woman with the man-child, the firstfruits and the harvest, the overcomers, the bride, the army, and the New Jerusalem. We should bring these eight signs to the Lord and pray-read all the related verses.

Because of the wrong concept in Christianity, most Christians consider that Revelation is too difficult for anyone to understand. For their entire life, many Christians do not get into the book of Revelation. If we still hold on to this concept, we have been drugged. May the Lord cause us to be sober. The book of Revelation is not too difficult. It simply presents the testimony of Jesus, which is the church as the corporate expression of Christ. We all know what a lampstand is. It is something that shines over us when we are in darkness. The great multitude of the redeemed in chapter 7 serve God in the heavenly temple and enjoy God's care and the Lamb's shepherding. The wonderful woman in chapter 12, clothed with the sun, the moon underneath her feet, and a crown of twelve stars upon her head, is the totality of God's people on earth. The church is also God's farm to grow Christ (1 Cor. 3:9). On this farm, those who ripen earlier are considered the firstfruits, and the rest are the harvest. The overcomers on the glassy sea in Revelation 15 are those who overcome the beast and all the negative things. Then in chapter 19, the church is not a harlot but a pure and bright bride, and it is the overcoming army to fight with Christ against Antichrist and his armies. Eventually we have the New Jerusalem in chapter 21. The New Jerusalem is altogether wonderful, so we need much understanding concerning it. In brief, the church as the testimony of Jesus is the lampstands, the multitude of the redeemed, the wonderful woman with the man-child, the farm to grow the firstfruits and the harvest, the overcomers, the bride, the army, and the New Jerusalem. In this testimony, Jesus is fully expressed and revealed. Therefore, in order to know Jesus and see such a Christ, we must come to the church.

This brief summary covers the entire book of Revelation. Some may say, "These are only seven chapters. What about the others?" The other chapters simply speak of horses, locusts, scorpions, frogs, beasts, a dragon, a serpent, and a great harlot. The great Babylon is in the category of the frogs, locusts, serpent, and dragon, but the New Jerusalem is in the category of the lampstands, the wonderful woman, the farm to grow Christ, and the overcomers. All the smaller items are the background and environment of the main picture, which is Christ as the Lion of the tribe of Judah (5:5). Nothing can defeat this Lion, neither the serpent, nor the frogs, nor the locusts. To us, the Lion is the redeeming Lamb, but to the enemy, the Lamb is the overcoming Lion. Moreover, He is fully expressed in the lampstand, the multitude of the redeemed, the woman with the man-child, the farm, the overcomers, the bride, the army, and the New Jerusalem. Through this summary, the entire book of Revelation should be open to all of us.

THE CHURCHES BEING THE SHINING, GOLDEN LAMPSTANDS

The lampstands are golden, not wooden or muddy. In typology, gold signifies the divine nature of God. The church must have the divine nature of God. We have all been born of God, and we have His life and nature (John 3:15; 2 Pet. 1:4). Therefore, we do have some amount of gold within us. Now we need to forsake our muddy and wooden nature and go along with the golden nature. We only need to listen to the God who lives, works, moves, and operates in us. If we would care for the divine nature, we will be golden. Other metals rust, but gold never rusts. It always remains the same. Likewise, the divine nature does not change; it remains forever the same. We do have this divine nature within us. Therefore, we should not develop our natural talents or natural being. Rather, we should cast them away and develop the divine nature within us to have the golden lampstands.

Moreover, the church is a stand, not something flat. The church is not low; it rises up and stands. The church must rise up higher than everything else. Those who are defeated and dead lie down, but as the church we must stand as the golden lampstand. We stand not by our nature, natural being, or natural talent but by God's divine nature. Many of our co-workers in mainland China, faithful ones with whom I worked for many years, were martyred. Recently, a co-worker who was learning under me since 1936 was martyred. The Communists demanded that people not talk about Jesus, but he protested in print that he must speak about Him. Because of this, the Communists killed him. To be sure, all these co-workers were standing as the testimony of Jesus.

We do not need a lampstand in the daytime. It is in the night that we need the lampstand to shine. The church must be golden, standing, and shining. Some people argue, "Are you the only church? Are we not the church?" Those who argue should simply check whether they are shining or darkened. When we come into a certain Christian meeting, do we see light there or is that meeting in darkness? The church shines; it is the shining lampstand. If we have been wrong with our wife, for example, when we come into the proper church, the light will shine on us. We will be exposed, our conscience will be enlightened and touched, and we will have the deep conviction that we should not be wrong in this way. If this is our experience, we can be assured that the place we are in is the church. On the other hand, if we come here again and again with no conviction that we are wrong with our wife, we are still in darkness, and the place in which we are is not the genuine church. The church is shining. Therefore, do not be careless in the church. Nothing exposes people as much as the church does. There is no need for anyone to speak frankly to us. When we simply come to the church, the light is there. The light comes from all around and embraces us, and we cannot escape it. If we try to run away, the light follows us and brings us back. Even if we do not like being exposed, we come back to be exposed again. Then we receive mercy, and grace follows. This is the experience of the church. The church is golden, the church is standing, and the church is shining. It is the golden lampstand.

In some places that claim to be the church, even the elders fight with one another. On the one hand, they say that they meet in the Lord's name and that they are the church, but on the other hand, they fight. This is not the church; it is a place of darkness. The church is a place where not only do we not fight, but even as we are about to lose our temper, we say, "O Lord, forgive me. Lord, I am so wrong." The church is the most exposing place. No man controls us here, but there is a King in the church. The Lord Jesus, not any of the elders, is the King. Many times the elders are very kind. They go along with us and say everything is fine. However, even if the elders say, "Fine," Jesus may say, "No." The elders may let us go, but Jesus would not let us go. He is the light, and He shines over us. If there is not this kind of light where we are, we should go elsewhere. We should not stay in a place where there is no light. Sometimes I have not spoken kindly with the elders, but I could go only so far in my speaking. I dared not go further, because the light shined within me. When I was about to speak too strongly, the light came, and I said, "O Lord Jesus! Cleanse me. Lord, I apply Your blood." Likewise, if we still can fight with our husband or wife for an extended time, we are not in the church in a practical way. I do not say that no one among us fights. It is just that after fighting for only a few minutes, King Jesus shines over us and within us to cause us to repent and confess. Because of this, we can say that we are in the church as the shining golden lampstand.

THE MULTITUDE OF THE REDEEMED SERVING GOD IN THE HEAVENLY TEMPLE

The great multitude in Revelation 7:9-17 consists of the redeemed ones from the nations throughout all generations, who are innumerable and who constitute the church. That they are standing before the throne indicates that they have been raptured to the heavens, to the presence of God. Thus, the record in these verses describes in a general way the scene from the time of the rapture of the believers to their enjoyment in eternity.

Verse 14 says, "These are those who come out of the great tribulation." The great tribulation here is different from the great tribulation mentioned in Matthew 24:21. The great tribulation here is tribulation in a general sense. All of God's redeemed people have passed through certain tribulations, sufferings, persecutions, and afflictions. No Christian can avoid these things. In our spirit, we Christians are a people of enjoyment, but on the physical side, we are a suffering people. However, one day we shall come triumphantly out of the great tribulation and stand before the Lamb. The palm branches in the hands of the saints signify their victory over tribulation, which they have undergone for the Lord's sake, and they are also a sign of satisfaction gained through being watered (Exo. 15:27). In eternity, the One who sits on the throne will tabernacle over them, overshadowing them with Himself as the One who is embodied in Christ (John 1:14). Moreover, they will not hunger or thirst any more, for the Lamb who is in the midst of the throne will shepherd them and guide them to springs of waters of life.

THE UNIVERSAL, BRIGHT WOMAN BEING THE TOTALITY OF ALL GOD'S PEOPLE

As we have seen, Revelation 12 speaks of a wonderful woman who delivers a man-child. She is universal and full of light. A lampstand needs to shine, but this woman has no need of shining; she is altogether in the light. Every kind of light bearer—the sun, the moon, and the stars—is around her. She is clothed with the sun, the moon is underneath her feet, and on her head is a crown of twelve stars. With her there is no day and night, because both the light bearer of the day and the light bearers of the night are with her, just as in the New Jerusalem there is no day or night because God's glory constantly shines within it (21:23). With this woman there is not one bit of darkness. I have seen the church in this kind of condition. The church is the shining lampstand, but in some places the church eventually becomes like this wonderful woman. How we thank the Lord that in these days the church is shining in this way.

If we have the spiritual eyes, we can see the situation of the church today. The church is a wonderful "woman" in our locality who will deliver a man-child to bring in the kingdom age and rule over all the nations. This picture is better than a thousand words. If we see this wonderful woman, we can understand where the church is and what the church is. This woman is universal. Likewise, we are in our locality, but we are universal. We are practical in order to be real in our city, but our nature is not of our city. Therefore, we do not use rock music, dramas, dancing, or anything else of this evil age. We use only that which is universal, bright, and full of light. This is the nature of the church as the testimony of Jesus today. The church is not only a shining lampstand. It also has the shining of the sun, the moon, and the stars. If we need light, we can come to the church. Many of us can testify that when we came to the church, it was as if the stars were over us, the moon was underneath our feet, and we were clothed, wrapped up, with the sun. Therefore, we could not escape. In this aspect, the church is not merely a lampstand, a light bearer; it is clothed with the universal light bearers. The light is concentrated in the church; outside the church there is no light.

For this reason, this is the place that the dragon hates. Before this universal woman is the great dragon ready to devour the man-child she brings forth (12:3-4). This indicates a spiritual battle. A dragon is greater than a serpent. This shows that Satan hates this woman with her man-child and will do everything he can to damage, swallow, and devour them. However, he cannot do it. Instead, he is cast down from the heaven to the earth by the very man-child who is delivered by the woman. We have the assurance that the man-child will be produced in the proper churches. We cannot expect Catholicism or the denominations to produce the man-child. Only a wonderful woman in light can deliver the man-child who will cast Satan down from the heavens to the earth. Eventually, the kingdom, the authority, of Christ will be ushered in by the man-child delivered by this bright woman. This is the testimony of Jesus.

THE CHURCH BEING GOD'S FARM TO PRODUCE THE FIRSTFRUITS AND THE HARVEST

The church is also a farm to grow Christ (1 Cor. 3:9). I was in Christianity for many years, but I had no growth there, because I had no life. A person can sit in the pews of certain denominations for many years, but year after year he will remain the same. However, if we attend the church meetings for only a few weeks, something within us will begin to grow and sprout. If we were all here according to our condition in the past, we would be a room full of locusts, scorpions, frogs, snakes, and beasts, but instead, many are here today as glowing and shining persons. It is the life within us that makes us this way. Something within us is growing, because the church is God's farm. Some on this farm will be the firstfruits. They will ripen first because they are growing more quickly. They are not defiled, and they follow the Lamb wherever He goes (Rev. 14:4). The condition for growing quickly is to follow the Lamb. Wherever He goes, we follow Him, and by following Him we grow more quickly. Then we will be the firstfruits. Nevertheless, even those who grow more slowly will still ripen to be the harvest.

The function of a farm is to produce food. The church is the place that God needs to produce food. When many of us were in the denominations, we received no food. In the church, however, there is much food. In the local churches today there is no dearth or famine. Rather, every local church is full of food. Recently, in a certain locality the sisters fed some of us up to five meals a day. Every meal was full of the riches of America, and I was fully nourished. The churches today are like this. Because message after message is one "dish" after another, we all need a large capacity and a strong digestion. This illustrates the aspect of the church as the farm to produce every kind of proper food.

THE OVERCOMERS REJOICING ON THE GLASSY SEA

In Revelation 15 the overcomers are standing on the glassy sea. Recently we have had many baptisms. The place of baptism may be considered as an entry to send all the negative things to the lake of fire. A sea should be of water, but the glassy sea is mingled with fire (v. 2). Water and fire together signify God's judgment throughout the entire Bible. God first judged His rebellious creatures with a flood of water. He judged the preadamic age with water, and He judged the age of Noah also with water (Gen. 1:2; 7:11-12, 21-23). After the flood, God told Noah that never again would there be a flood to destroy the earth (9:15). Nevertheless, the Bible tells us that God continued His judgment with fire. The glassy sea is a final symbol of God's judgment by water and fire.

The flood at Noah's time may be considered a kind of baptism (1 Pet. 3:20-21). The crossing of the Red Sea (Exo. 14:16-31), the laver in the tabernacle (30:17-21), and the bronze sea with the ten bronze lavers in the temple (1 Kings 7:23-40a) were also types of baptism. In the New Testament, John the Baptist told people to be buried in water (Mark 1:4; Matt. 3:5-6), and throughout the entire Christian era, many Christians have been baptized. Worldly things, sinful things, the flesh, and everything else negative goes into the water and eventually into the lake of fire (Rev. 20:14-15). Therefore, in front of God there is a sea of glass mingled with fire, and the overcomers are on the seashore, just as the Israelites stood on the shore, dancing, rejoicing, and singing after passing through the Red Sea. This signifies that in the church life we do not keep anything negative; everything negative must go.

After being buried in baptism and getting rid of all the negative things, many believers, in principle, dance and sing the song of Moses and the song of the Lamb. All the negative things are under their feet, and they are on the seashore. Today we are on the shore of the glassy sea, where all the negative things go on their way to the lake of fire. We are cleansed and pure, and every negative thing is gone. Therefore, we are the overcomers, and the world is under our feet. The world, the modern fashion, and the department stores are all in the glassy sea. We say to all the negative things, "Go to that sea. Get away from me and my home." We are the cleansed people, the baptized people, those who rise up from the judging waters and are now on the seashore.

Whenever we come together, we should have the sensation that we are on the shore of the glassy sea. The worldly attraction of the department stores and the worldly entertainment of television are in the glassy sea on the way to the lake of fire, but we are on the shore dancing, rejoicing, and singing. We are baptized, released, and resurrected. We are meeting not under the sea but on the seashore. When we were in the denominations, we were "under the sea." We could not shout, rejoice, or sing. The proper church life, however, is on the seashore. Those who meet in the proper church are able to stand on the glassy sea. This is the experience of the church.

THE BRIDE BEING THE EXPRESSION OF CHRIST IN THE MILLENNIUM

The bride in Revelation 19 is what the church will be in the millennium, the thousand-year kingdom. A thousand years to God are one day (2 Pet. 3:8). Therefore, the millennium will be a wedding day. On the wedding day the female is the bride; following this, the bride becomes the wife. The church in the millennium will be the bride, and the entire thousand years will be the wedding day with the wedding feast. An American wedding feast may last only half an hour, but a Chinese wedding feast may last much longer. The Chinese truly know how to enjoy a wedding feast by eating, drinking, talking, and rejoicing for four or five hours. However, this is still too short. The bride will have a wedding feast that will last one thousand years.

The bride is clothed in fine linen, bright and clean (Rev. 19:8). In the Bible, white linen typifies Christ as our righteousness. Christ is righteousness to us in two aspects. First, we receive Him as our objective righteousness for our salvation. Then after this, we need to live Him out as our subjective righteousness. This second aspect of righteousness is not for our salvation but for our prize in the millennial kingdom (Phil. 3:9, 14; 1 Cor. 9:24). The white linen that the bride wears is not the Christ whom we receive initially but the Christ whom we live out. Not all Christians will be the bride in the thousand years. Only those who live out Christ as their subjective righteousness will be the bride.

THE OVERCOMING ARMY TO DEFEAT THE ENEMIES OF CHRIST

The armies in Revelation 19:14 are the called and chosen believers in 17:14 and those who are called to the marriage dinner of the Lamb in 19:9, that is, those who constitute the bride of Christ. After the marriage dinner of the Lamb, the bride will become the army. Verse 14 says that the armies are dressed in fine linen, white and clean. The overcoming saints have two garments. The first garment is Christ as our objective righteousness for our justification (Luke 15:22; Psa. 45:13), and the second is Christ lived out of us to be our daily, subjective righteousness (Matt. 22:11-12; 5:20; Psa. 45:14; Rev. 3:4-5, 18). The first garment is for our salvation, but the second is for our reward. The fine linen in Revelation 19:8 and 14 is the second garment, which qualifies the overcomers both to attend the marriage dinner of the Lamb and to fight with the Lord against His enemy. Thus, the wedding garment becomes the fighting garment.

In Revelation 19, the enemies of Christ are Antichrist, the kings of the earth, and their armies. The war in verses 19 through 21 will take place at Armageddon, at the valley of Jehoshaphat (Joel 3:9-16; Zech. 14:2-3, 12-15), which is very close to Jerusalem, and it will be the treading of the great winepress of the fury of God (Rev. 14:17-20). As the result of this war, Christ will defeat Antichrist, who, with the false prophet, will be cast alive into the lake of fire. Then the rest of Antichrist's armies will be killed with the sword that proceeds out of the mouth of Christ, who is the King of kings and Lord of lords (19:16).

THE NEW JERUSALEM BEING THE FULLEST, ULTIMATE TESTIMONY OF JESUS

After the millennial kingdom, the New Jerusalem as the totality of all God's chosen and redeemed people will appear. In the thousand years the bride wears fine linen, but in eternity the New Jerusalem will be built with jasper (21:18-19). In the Old Testament the tabernacle was covered with white linen. However, this was something temporary, not eternal. After the tabernacle there was the temple, which was built no longer with linen but with precious stones. In the millennium, the overcomers as the bride will express Christ as their white linen. They will have no mixture, spot, or anything dirty, but everything will be bright, clean, and pure. That is a picture of the Christ whom we live out. However, this also will be a temporary situation. Eventually, we will all come to the final aspect of the testimony of Jesus. We will be the New Jerusalem in eternity, expressing God no longer only as white linen but as precious, glowing, shining jasper.

Step after step and aspect after aspect, the testimony of Jesus begins with the lampstands, passes through the great multitude, the universal, bright woman, the firstfruits and harvest, the overcomers on the glassy sea, the bride, and the army, and it finally comes to the New Jerusalem, where Christ is fully expressed and testified. The New Jerusalem will be the testimony of Jesus in the fullest, ultimate way. God is expressed in Christ, Christ is expressed in the New Jerusalem, and the New Jerusalem is the ultimate consummation of the church. This is the revelation of Christ, and this is the testimony of Jesus.

All of the above fellowship should help us to see what the church is. It is not satanic Judaism, demonic Catholicism, lifeless and Christless Protestantism, or devilish worldliness, with all the locusts, scorpions, frogs, beasts, serpent, dragon, and Babylon the Great, which will fall and be cast into the lake of fire. Rather, it is the corporate testimony of Jesus. Therefore, to practice the church life is not simply to meet in the name of the Lord on the proper ground of the church. We must also have the reality of the testimony of Jesus as the shining lampstand, the multitude serving God in the heavenly temple, the wonderful woman to produce the man-child, the field that grows the firstfruits and harvest, the overcomers on the glassy sea, the bride expressing Christ as the white linen, the overcoming army to defeat Antichrist, and the New Jerusalem as the full expression and testimony of Jesus. This is the genuine church life. May we all see this vision.